The
Cockatiel
Handbook

Matthew M. Vriends, Ph.D.

With Color Photography
Drawings by Michele Earle-Bridges

BARRON'S

Photo Credits
   B. Everett Webb: pages vi, 4, 5, 7 top left, 8, 9, 17 top right,
20 top left, 21 bottom right, 22, 28, 31, 32, 53, 64, 67, 68, 73,
79, 85, 92, 93, 96, 122, 124 bottom left, 132, 137, 139, 142
top left, 142 bottom left, 142 top right, 143, 145, 146 top left,
150 bottom left, 166, 171; Pieter van den Hooven: pages vii,
6 top right, 6 top left, 15 bottom right, 21 top left, 141,
146 top right, 147, 149, 150 bottom right, 151, 152, 153 bottom right, 154, 157, 168, 170; Matthew Vriends: pages viii, 3,
6 top left, 11, 12, 17 bottom right, 18, 20 bottom left, 21 top
right, 23 bottom left, 23 bottom right, 25, 37, 70, 76, 80, 81,
83, 84, 86, 88, 110, 111, 119, 121 top left, 123 top right, 123
bottom right, 124 top left, 126, 142 bottom right, 153 bottom
left, 164, 173; Jan Blasman: pages 1, 10 top right, 27, 29,
120, 121 top right; Joan Balzarini: pages 2, 7 top right, 10 top
left, 14, 15 top right, 23 top right, 30, 46, 49, 127, 138, 155;
B. van de Kamer: pages: 162, 163.

Cover Photos
   B. Everett Webb

All inquiries should be addressed to:
Barron's Educational Series, Inc.
250 Wireless Boulevard
Hauppauge, New York 11788
http://www.barronseduc.com

International Standard Book No. 0-7641-1017-9
Library of Congress Catalog Card No. 99-19206

Library of Congress Cataloging-in-Publication Data
Vriends, Matthew M., 1937–.
   The cockatiel handbook : everything about purchase,
housing, care, nutrition, behavior, breeding, and diseases,
with a special chapter on breeding cockatiels / Matthew
M. Vriends ; color photos by well-known photographers
and drawings by Michele Earl-Bridges.
      p.   cm.
   Rev. ed. of: New cockatiel handbook. ©1989.
   Includes bibliographical references (p.   ) and index.
   ISBN 0-7641-1017-9
   1. Cockatiel. I. Vriends, Matthew M., 1937– New
cockatiel handbook. II. Title.
SF473.C6V745   1999
636.6'8656—dc21   99-19206
                                        CIP

Printed in Hong Kong

9 8 7 6 5 4

About the Author
   Matthew M. Vriends is a Dutch-born biologist/ornitholo-
gist who holds a collection of advanced degrees, including
a PhD in zoology. Dr. Vriends has written more than 100
books in three languages on birds and other animals; his
detailed works on parrotlike birds and finches are well
known. Dr. Vriends has traveled extensively in South
America, the United States, Africa, Australia, and Europe to
observe and study birds in their natural environment and is
widely regarded as an expert in tropical ornithology and
aviculture. A source of particular pride are the many first-
breeding results he has achieved in his large aviaries, which
house more than 50 tropical bird species. Dr. Vriends lives
on Long Island, New York. He is the author of seven
Barron's Pet Owner's Manuals, *Hedgehogs, Lovebirds,*
Pigeons, Conures, Lories and Lorikeets, Doves, and
Gouldian Finches. He is also the author of Barron's
Complete Nature Lover's Manual, *Feeding and Sheltering*
Backyard Birds, and of Barron's *The New Australian*
Parakeet Handbook, The New Bird Handbook, The New
Canary Handbook, Hand-Feeding and Raising Baby Birds,
and *The Parrotlet Handbook.*

Important Note
The subject of this book is how to take care of cockatiels
in captivity. In dealing with these birds, always remember
that newly purchased birds—even when they appear
perfectly healthy—may well be carriers of salmonellae.
This is why it is highly advisable to have sample droppings analyzed and to observe strict hygienic rules. Other
infectious diseases that can endanger humans, such as
ornithosis and tuberculosis, are rare in cockatiels. Still, if
you see a doctor because you or a member of your
household has symptoms of a cold or of the flu, mention
that you keep birds. No one who is allergic to feathers or
feather dust should keep birds. If you have any doubts,
consult your physician before you buy a bird.
   Many insects used as food by birds are pests that can
infest stored food and create a serious nuisance in our
households. If you decide to grow any of these insects,
be extremely careful to prevent them from escaping
from their containers.

Contents

Preface   vi

1. Considerations Before Purchasing   1
Do You Really Want to Keep Cockatiels?   1
Do Cockatiels Fit Your Way of Life?   4
Obtaining Cockatiels   7
Welcome Home!   13
The First Few Weeks   17

2. Housing, Care, and Management   19
Cages   19
The Aviary   26
The Bird Room   37
Location of Cages and Aviaries   38
Plantings   40
Keeping the Cage Clean   45
Basic Grooming   46
Special Care Considerations   48
Table of Dangers   50

3. Foods and Feeding   52
Proteins   52
Carbohydrates   54
Fats and Oils   54
Vitamins   55
Minerals   59
Water   61
Green Food   62
Seeds   64
The Most Important Seeds   68
Rearing Food   73
Concentrated or Universal Food   73

Insects 74
Fruit 74
Table Scraps 74
Bird Pellets/Extruded Diets 75
Cleanliness and Hygiene 76
Conclusion 76

4. Taming and Training **78**
The First Steps 78
Outside the Cage 79
T Perch Training 81
The Ladder 82
Tricks 85
Wing Clipping 86
The Talking Cockatiel 87

5. If Your Cockatiel Gets Sick **94**
The First Steps 94
Hospital Cages 95
What to Look For 96
Preventive Care 99
Diseases and Injuries 99
Basic Medications 116
Other Health Necessities 117

6. Breeding Cockatiels **119**
Introduction 119
Choosing Breed Stock 119
The Nest Box 120
The Eggs 124
The Nestlings 127
Banding 128
Trouble-shooting 129
Pointers for Breeders 130
Worming the Fledglings 131
Chronology 131
Caring for Young Cockatiels 132
Abandoned Eggs 134
Incubating Eggs 134
Hand-rearing 136

7. Heredity and Mutations   **141**

Colors   141
Mutations   143
Principles of Heredity   148
Formulas   149
Crossing Mutations   157
Additional Considerations   157

8. Understanding Cockatiels   **158**

Physical Characteristics   158
Feathers   159
Distribution   161
The Cockatiel in the Wild   162
Flight   165
Breeding   165
The Cockatiel in Scientific Literature   167
How Cockatiels Came to Europe and the United States   170
The American Cockatiel Society (ACS) Show Standard   172
Bands   175
ACS Point Standard   175

Useful Addresses and Literature   **177**

Index   **179**

Preface

As I write these words, I can look across my desk and observe a large cage containing a pair of normal gray cockatiels. These two slender, cheerful birds, which are enjoying a well-earned rest after the breeding season, have free access to my entire study. Their cage door is never closed.

These cockatiels were my first pair, and I carefully hand-reared them some nine years ago. They are still the only birds (and I now have about 200) that spend the winter months in my study. They are the proud parents of about 65 young, the grandparents of hundreds, and the great-grandparents of many thousands of cockatiels. I have remained devoted to these birds; perhaps I am addicted to them—who knows? In any case, a sort of true and faithful friendship has developed between us. I now have another 20 or more pairs in all manner of color varieties, but it is this pair of "old" birds that has really stolen my heart.

I have often asked myself why cockatiels are so appealing. Along with budgerigars and canaries, they are the most popular cage birds in the world. To answer this question I have prepared a list of their most endearing characteristics; you will certainly be able to add to it.

• Their attractive colors and patterns, cute crests, and graceful bodies.

• Their convivial behavior, friendly personality, adaptability, and capacity to learn to talk and whistle.

• The relative ease with which they will mate and raise their young in a large breeding cage, a room aviary, or (especially) in a garden aviary.

It is a well-known fact that cockatiels (Nymphicus hollandicus) *make excellent aviary and cage birds, and even a beginner should have little difficulty in keeping a pair (or even more!). Not only are they endowed with beautiful coloring, but with a noble crest and a fine build as well, making them great favorites among aviculturists the world over.*

• The possibility that one or more pairs will breed at the same time in the same aviary.

• Their willingness to be housed with other seed-eating birds (as long as other species of parakeets and parrots are not included).

• Their longevity.

Indeed, cockatiels are a most attractive species. Over the years, my experience with them has reinforced all of these points many times.

This book is based on the many years of my experiences with captive cockatiels, as well as the opportunities I have had to observe and study these charming birds in their native environment. Many of the points discussed in this book originated from correspondence with enthusiasts from around the world.

In this book I will endeavor to answer many, but by no means all, of the questions one might ask about cockatiels. Who would be qualified to do that?

Like their masters, cockatiels have many sides to their character. The love of a breeder for his other birds and the joy that this love begets will influence the birds. To love means to care, and caring will be appreciated and reciprocated.

Raising cockatiels is a pleasurable, educational, and relaxing hobby, the value of which can be appreciated only by those who participate. These birds are marvelous breeders. Some regard this willingness of the birds to cooperate with an eye to profit; some, just as a

In a class by himself is, in the cockatiel's case, fact as much as praise. Because of his unique structure, scientists have classified this enchanting bird into a separate genus and species, Nymphicus hollandicus. *However science regards him, his ever-growing legion of friends find in the cockatiel all the pleasure anyone would seek in a pet bird.*

Cockatiels stand out because of their decorative crest. They are also excellent breeders and outstanding foster parents (especially for the little Australian grass parakeets). The picture shows a female.

When a bird species has various color mutations it is always possible through a series of matings to produce birds that show the characteristics of two or more mutations in one bird, and our cockatiels are no exception to this rule.

means to reimburse the cost of feeding and housing them.

Those who keep birds for the sake of the birds will improve their own quality of life. Bird fanciers know this from experience, and it is their task to act as ambassadors for the hobby. Give a pair of cockatiels (or sell them for a few dollars—not the full price) to a friend, acquaintance, or relative; a hospital, school, or nursing home. Tell them about the birds, give advice and help in the construction of an aviary, or the purchase of good equipment. Then see how many cockatiel friends you have made!

This book has been written in the hope that it will arouse an interest in cockatiels in many newcomers to the hobby. It is also written by one cockatiel fancier in the hope that it will be of benefit to other cockatiel fanciers.

I wish to thank my friend Arthur Freud for taking time from his busy schedule to review the manuscript, and for the valuable contributions he has made to the text. My heartfelt thanks go also to my friend, John Coborn of Queensland, Australia, for the work he has taken off my hands. My daughter, Tanya Heming-Vriends, I thank for her moral support and her editorial and ornithological expertise. Last, but by no means least, I thank my friend Tom Squyres of Fort Worth, Texas, and Rogert G. Heroux of West Palm Beach, Florida, founder and past-president of the American Cockatiel Society, Inc., respectively, for providing the information on their show standards. It goes without saying, however, that any faults or omissions in the text are my own responsibility.

As always, I will be grateful for any comments or constructive criticism on the contents of the text of this revised edition.

Matthew M. Vriends
Long Island, New York
Summer 1999

Soyons fidèles à nos faiblesses.

For Kimy and Korrina Lindsey, my beautiful grandchildren, and their mother, my lovely daughter Tanya, and Eddie, my fine son-in-law.

Chapter One
Considerations Before Purchasing

Do You Really Want to Keep Cockatiels?

I strongly recommend that you do not consider keeping cockatiels "just as something to do." If you do not have the necessary enthusiasm, it is best not to become involved with aviculture.

But if you have a love of birds in general and cockatiels in particular, and if you have the essential patience, understanding, and enthusiasm, then it is possible that you may become a true cockatiel fancier!

Keeping cockatiels costs money. The amount depends upon you. If you decide at the outset to buy several cages and to have aviaries built to order from the best possible material, then your new hobby can become extremely expensive.

But if you start off modestly, cockatiel keeping really need not cost *that* much. So long as you do not have two left hands, you can build your own breeding cages; and

the price of one or two pairs of birds is not going to break you.

If you barter or sell the young you breed and use the money to buy better stock, you will improve the standard of your stud and possibly be able to afford to build better aviaries.

As long as you restrict yourself to one or two pairs, you should be able

A beautiful breeding pair of gray (or normal) colored cockatiels as they appear in the wild habitats of Australia.

to manage your feeding budget comfortably—even allowing for extra rearing food in the breeding season.

In time, you will master the hobby and become a fully qualified breeder. At this point, if you have the necessary spare time and space, making a modest profit is not out of the question. And theoretically, over the years, it may even be possible to make a significant sum from the sale of cockatiels.

I say "theoretically" because the actual outcome may be quite different. Consider the example of a hobbyist friend of mine who, at age 65, retired from his job as a teacher. With many years of breeding experience behind him, he decided to undertake a large breeding project.

The man took no risks. He had everything carefully worked out: the cost of the cages and aviaries, the cost of foodstuffs, the work involved, and the average price he would have to charge for young birds to make a profit. Even the cost of extra heating and lighting in winter and an allowance for occasional extraordinary veterinary fees were included in his figures. His careful reckoning showed that he should make about $1,200 per annum from ten breeding pairs of birds and that, in a good year, he could clear more than $2,000.

After four years, the man shut up shop. In the first year, he broke even; in the second year, he made $800; in the third year, he lost $400; and in the fourth year, he again broke even. So, for four years of hard work, he had made just $400.

However, he was not a disappointed man. For four years he had worked hard and experimented with his hobby. Although he had done little to supplement his income, the enjoyment he derived from working with his birds had helped him to remain keen and vigorous.

No, the true rewards of the cockatiel fancy cannot be reckoned in terms of monetary gain. And if the love of the hobby does not come first, then the pleasure will be lost. Anyone who looks at birds as investments is totally on the wrong track.

This does not mean that, as you breed your cockatiels and build up a valuable stock, you may not find that you have surplus birds. Then, obviously, it becomes a question of trying to get the best possible price for them. With luck, you can sometimes make a nice little profit with cockatiels.

Regard such a profit as a windfall, however. If you expect it to become the rule, the true value of your hobby will be lost.

Indeed, some breeders may never have surplus stock. Most of the men and women who breed color mutations would rather have a few beautiful birds than many ordinary ones. These are the pure hobbyists, who do not take profit into consideration or even think about it. They are, perhaps, the happiest in the hobby; to them, it remains what it should be—a splendid pastime.

There are many other types of hobbyists: the man who gets great enjoyment from keeping a single cockatiel in a cage; the teenager who keeps a small breeding aviary on a balcony; the woman who keeps a breeding cage in her den, where she can wonder at the brooding and

People are finding out that cockatiels are very easy to train, and of course their cost is very reasonable when compared with many other members of the parrot family.

rearing of new lives. Each has found his or her own way of enjoying the birds and probably gets as much pleasure as the person with a hundred cockatiels.

Young hens can be trained and many will make affectionate pets, like this female bird, and learn how to talk. Young males are less temperamental and usually learn to talk with greater ease.

Do Cockatiels Fit Your Way of Life?

Keeping one or more cockatiels—or indeed any other kind of bird—requires a great deal of consideration. Besides the initial and ongoing costs, which have been mentioned, you must also remember that the keeping of cockatiels is a long-term commitment; cockatiels over 12 years of age are by no means uncommon!

There are additional aspects that are worth considering in advance. Examine yourself carefully, and be sure to discuss these relevant points with your family:

• Cockatiels are messy. If you have a cage in the house, water will be splashed around, along with seed

If cockatiels are kept in cages all the time they tend to deteriorate in general quality and in breeding potential. Therefore, give them the opportunity to fly free in the room on a daily basis, supervised, of course.

husks, loose feathers, and similar detritus. Are you prepared to be confronted with this each day—and to clean it up?

• Because cockatiels are not particularly "tidy" birds, the food and water dishes will have to be cleaned daily; the cage must be thoroughly cleaned at least once per week and the perches scraped and sanded as required. And every two weeks cage and utensils must be disinfected.

• Are you prepared to collect fresh twigs of willow and other trees regularly so that your birds can have fresh treats to munch?

• Are you prepared to give your birds fresh food and drink every day (including Saturdays and Sundays), and this preferably at the same time each day so that the birds become accustomed to routine?

• Are you prepared to become a member of a bird club (where you will learn much that will benefit your birds)?

• Is there somebody you can rely on to look after your birds if you are sick or away on vacation?

• Is there an avian veterinarian in your area whom you can consult if your birds become sick?

• If you intend to breed cockatiels, are you prepared to accommodate your birds in proper breeding cages and aviaries (and not some old box you may have picked up at a garage sale)? Have you enough space for proper cages and aviaries?

• If you live in a rented house or apartment, what will your landlord say about your birds?

These nice-looking lutino cockatiels have a roomy cage. Cages for housing a single breeding pair or half a dozen birds for steadying down for show purposes should be approximately 4 ft (1.3 m) in length by 6 ft (2 m) wide and 3 ft (1 m) high.

This is the attractive cockatiel aviary of the Capitol City Bird Society (CA). It is a good idea to become a member of a bird club: you will learn much that will benefit your birds and there will always be somebody you can rely on to look after your birds if you are sick or away on vacation.

• Even well-adjusted cockatiels sometimes screech (especially early in the morning and at dusk), so it is best to get the cooperation of your neighbors. If you live in an apartment or if you intend to build aviaries in your garden, this must be done before you acquire any birds.

A Single Cockatiel or a Pair?

If you decide to buy just one bird, consider the fact that, without another member of its own species, your pet will become very dependent on you. Like it or not, you will be the surrogate partner. This responsibility will take considerable time. If your bird is left on its own for most of the day, you may have a neurotic animal in no time at all. Under stress it may develop all sorts of bad habits such as screeching and feather plucking.

Cockatiels and Other Pets

Do you have other pets in the house? This can raise problems. Dogs, especially hunting breeds, can be carried into fits of excitement by a tame, free-flying cockatiel in the house, and cats are definite "no-nos." (In spite of the familiar stories about cats and birds becoming the best of friends, sooner or later the natural instincts of the cat may outweigh all other considerations. The unfortunate bird then becomes an item on the menu!)

Cockatiels and Children

A child can get a great deal of fun from having a cockatiel as a

Is there an avian veterinarian in your area whom you can consult if your birds become sick? Otherwise ask the American Federation of Aviculture or the Association of Avian Veterinarians (see page 177 for addresses).

A single male cockatiel of excellent carriage. If there is no partner you should be its friend and soulmate. At least two or three hours per day of interaction is essential and required—and if you can't realize this the singleton should have a bird partner without delay, and this doesn't have to be another cockatiel. A budgerigar (or budgie) will do fine!

A pair of cockatiels. Now you can leave them alone, knowing that your friends will not be bored or stressed.

companion, and the cockatiel, too, will certainly enjoy the relationship. As I have said, cockatiels are very affectionate, easily tamed, and always willing to play games. With their ability to learn to imitate the human voice, these birds are a constant delight.

Additionally, a pet cockatiel can be a great asset to a child's education. Not only can a child thus

Any child can get a great deal of fun from having a cockatiel as a companion, and the bird too will certainly enjoy the relationship.

A pearl pied cockatiel and its friend. Usually a cockatiel has a friendly, affectionate personality. However, it is not advisable to bring your pet too close to your face; a startling movement or noise could result in a painful nip.

become more aware of the wonders of nature, but by taking care of a bird, the child can learn a love for the natural world in general, and respect for all living things. In the modern world, filled with troubles and strife, taking care of birds can give one a great deal of spiritual and physical satisfaction. Indeed, the whole family can derive the greatest of pleasure by observing the tame cockatiel and the child together.

Obtaining Cockatiels

If you have serious intentions of breeding cockatiels, only the very best is good enough.

If you require only a single pet cockatiel in a cage, different standards apply. You can be quite happy with the character and color of a bird that is not champion material. Even in this case, however, you must be sure your bird is healthy.

At this point, let us consider the situation of people who intend to breed cockatiels. For them, the quality of the initial acquisitions is extremely important because these birds will be the bases of their breeding stock. These birds are the key factor in determining whether the future breeding program is to be a success or a failure, and thus will often have a bearing on whether the newcomer will become a "real" fancier or, after two or three years,

A slender wild or gray (normal) colored male cockatiel of approximately 8 months. In another 4 months it can be used in a breeding program. Best results, however, are obtained with birds that are somewhere between 24 and 26 months.

money can buy; you would learn on a pair of good, simple skates and gain proficiency before you went on to more ambitious projects, which would then warrant buying a more expensive pair. By the same token, if you are a beginning breeder, I recommend you start with a good pair of normal grays. They are not expensive and will not tax your knowledge; they will not have any problems as they are unlikely to be inbred; and, since they are bred in great numbers, they should not be difficult to obtain.

To be honest, many fanciers are not that enthusiastic about starting to breed cockatiels, nor will everyone turn into an enthusiastic breeder. If, after a couple of years, you find that you do not have enough "breeding blood," then all is not lost; nor will you have spent a lot of money.

In any case, the first birds you acquire must be regarded as study material. With them you can learn how to deal with birds in and out of the breeding season, how the young are reared, what problems may arise with housing, and all about the other facets of cockatiel raising. After a couple of seasons, when you have picked up the basics, the way is open for you to expand your interest in the hobby—or to pull back to a somewhat smaller commitment to your birds.

You should thus buy the best normal grays you can afford. Don't go in for runts; do buy the healthiest-looking birds you can find, even if they are a dollar or so more expensive.

become disillusioned and give it up as a bad job.

One might assume that it is therefore essential for a beginner to start with a pair of very special birds— "super" lutinos, for example, which are white birds with an even, delicate yellow cast over their bodies. This is not so. In fact, the novice would not know where to begin with such birds. Were you learning to skate, for example, you would not start with the most expensive skates

Where to Buy Cockatiels

Try to get your birds from a reputable dealer or breeder. If you do not know one, go to a bird society exhibition. You will be able to see the standard of birds expected on the bench and will be able to find out who the best breeders are.

Even better, join a society, where you will be able to obtain the best advice for buying birds. Do not be afraid to ask for advice before purchasing stock. As a novice you will not know the good and bad qualities of a bird, but an experienced fancier will know and will be willing to help you. By looking at a bird an alert birdkeeper can tell if it is in the best of health, if it is fit, and whether it is a cock or a hen. Experienced fanciers will also spot any signs of disease or disability. But whether you get advice or go it alone, do not restrict your attention to the birds.

Buy only from breeders or dealers who keep their cages and aviaries in the best of order. I once had an acquaintance who would inspect a restaurant's toilet before ordering lunch. His philosophy was that if the toilet was clean and tidy, then it was safe to eat the food. This also applies to our hobby; if a dealer's cages and aviaries are clean, tidy, and in good order, then one should have no worries in buying birds. The breeder or dealer is obviously conscientious in one aspect, thus is likely to be so in all others. The birds will be fit and healthy, well fed and cared for. However, if you come across an establishment with dirty,

You should buy only high quality birds as they will be the base of your breeding stock.

These birds are fit and healthy, and well fed and cared for. As a novice it is not always easy to know the good and bad qualities of a bird. When buying birds it is best to ask an experienced aviculturist to assist you in purchasing them.

A normal pearl, and a pied cockatiel—before you start breeding color mutations you should know at least the essentials of genetics.

White cockatiels with brown eyes are at this moment relatively easy to come by but are still rather high in price. This is a recessive mutation that resembles the albino but has dark brown instead of red eyes. At first glance the eyes look black. A mating of a normal gray male × a white bird with brown eyes gives 100 percent normal, all of which are split for white with brown eyes. White with brown eyes × split gives 50 percent white with brown eyes and 50 percent split for white with brown eyes.

untidy cages, aviaries, and sur-roundings, do not be tempted to buy any birds.

What to Look For

Good breeders will also have banded their birds for identification and will most probably keep a stud book, where they have recorded all sorts of information about each par-ticular bird in the stud. It is important to acquire birds born in spring or summer as these have the best chance for healthy development. (See page 13.) Such information will be found in the stud book.

Of course, you must also know what to look for in a healthy bird. A healthy bird will sit upright and nim-bly on its perch. It will have bright,

shiny eyes and smooth, sleek, tightly packed plumage. It will not allow itself to be harassed by other birds in the cage.

The cockatiel's eyes should be clear and bright, and there should be no dirt hanging from its feet or beak. When prospective purchasers observe birds, they usually stand next to the cages—after all, they want to see what they are buying close up. However, it's also a good idea to view birds from a moderate

Notwithstanding his Australian origin, the cockatiel is a hardy bird and can even thrive as an aviary bird in our colder states and Canada if properly conditioned. These normal grays are not even fazed by the snow on the wires of their aviary!

distance, preferably in their own "abode" and not in a small transport or observation cage.

When you approach too closely, a healthy bird is likely to show fear, flying away but still focusing its attention on you. A sick bird may walk or perhaps fly away, but it is more likely to show no interest at all. Don't be misled by the apparently "tame" nature of such a bird. Only birds that are agile, alert, and observant should be considered for purchase.

Healthy birds have a smooth coat of feathers. The tail feathers may be a little frayed along the edges, but this is usually a result of too small a cage or inadequate bathing facilities and, in itself, is no cause for concern.

Sometimes a bird will have one or more feathers missing. A common cause of feather loss is too much handling—for example, catching the bird and moving it from one cage to another too often. The feathers will be replaced at the next molt, but it's poor birdkeeping to grab birds more than is absolutely necessary. Missing feathers from a recently purchased bird are usually no cause for concern. Some cockatiels may have had their flight feathers clipped to prevent their flying heavily against the cage or aviary wire.

Take a likely-looking bird in your hand and examine it from beak to tail tip. The beak should close properly and be smooth in texture. Be sure there are no bald patches on top of its head. Check to see that there are no damaged wing feathers and that the tail is not soiled. Look at the feet one at a time; they should be clean and smooth. The toes must be straight and complete with claws: if the birds are old, you can often see calcium deposits.

The breastbone (sternum) runs down through the center of the breast. Palpate the (flight) muscles on either side of the breastbone; they should feel plump and firm, not hollow, with the breastbone showing through like a blade.

Look at the area around the vent. If it is dirty and matted with drop-pings or stains, the bird may be suffering from some kind of intestinal disorder. For obvious reasons, such birds should *not* be purchased.

Hold the bird to your ear and listen to its breathing. If you hear a squawking or rasping noise, the bird probably has a respiratory infection and should not be purchased.

Blow open the feathers on the breast. The skin you can see should look clean and healthy, not spotty or red.

If a bird looks good based on the above criteria, you can be pretty sure of getting a healthy specimen— and that is the primary purpose of this section of the book.

Naturally, we do not mean to indicate that the disease symptoms mentioned above are necessarily fatal to cockatiels. There are treatments for these and other ailments as you will see in the chapter on diseases. But, of course, beginners do not want to be plagued with problems of sickness in their birds at the very start.

The best advice can be summarized in an even dozen words: Never buy inferior material; buy the best and healthiest you can afford.

Cockatiels, like this pair of normal grays, are gentle birds with friendly personalities. They can be housed with many other seed-eating bird species. In this aviary they are living peacefully with budgerigars—a combination that cannot always be recommended (see page 26).

When to Buy Cockatiels

Theoretically, cockatiels can be bought at any time of the year. In practice, however, there are some problems that should always be taken into consideration.

In the first place, if you buy a cockatiel that has been kept in a heated indoor aviary in the late fall, winter, or early spring, you cannot set that bird outside immediately after purchase. It would quickly catch a cold or worse. This means that fanciers with outside aviaries should buy only birds from outside aviaries during the winter. The reverse presents no difficulty. Birds that are brought from a cold outdoors into a light, warm indoor place face no problem.

The best time for the average purchaser to acquire birds is thus in the late spring, summer, or early fall, when the difference between indoor and outdoor temperatures is not great enough to cause problems. However, late spring and summer present other problems. At these times, cockatiels are in short supply, as most birds are being used for breeding. Birds that may be offered for sale are likely to be weak individuals that, for some reason or other, are unsuitable for breeding. Thus, if possible, purchase birds in the fall. Temperature should present no problems, and you will have the greatest choice from among the birds bred in the preceding season.

Do not wait until too late in the fall before you buy. In the early part of fall, you will have the greatest choice from the first clutches of the season. These will be the best birds for breeding the next season, when they will be the right age. But if you buy late in the fall, the birds are likely to be from later clutches and will not be old enough to breed in the next season. Moreover, youngsters from later broods are usually somewhat

inferior in quality to the earlier birds.

The very best time to purchase birds, then, is in the early fall. This advice relates to birds from the breeders, most of whom sell their birds to pet shops. There are some breeders who wait until the spring before selling, so that they can ask a higher price, but one must remember that it costs money to keep and feed the birds through the winter, and there is a risk that some birds may die. It is thus logical for a breeder to dispose of all surplus birds in the fall or winter.

Welcome Home!

Once you have decided to purchase a cockatiel, you will face two important questions: How do you transport a young, untrained bird to its new home? How do you accustom the bird to its new surroundings as quickly as possible?

Transporting a Cockatiel

A bird should never be transported in a large, ornamental cage. Even if you were to wrap the cage in some sort of covering, the frightened bird would flap about and probably injure itself. Additionally, once the bird arrives in its new home, it will be exhausted and nervous from all the flapping about. All birds, including cockatiels, should be transported in a special traveling cage. Most retailers supply stout cardboard boxes of a size in which the bird can comfortably sit, somewhat restrained, but

This is a healthy-looking cinnamon pearl pied cockatiel. If you like to use play-ropes as perches, keep an extra eye out for the nails of your birds, for obvious reasons!

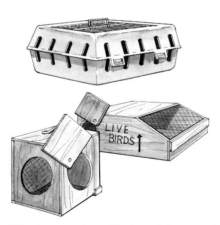

LIVE
BIRDS

Shipping containers. Each container must have openings to supply enough air for breathing. Never place bird containers on a section of the floor that is heated; overheating in the container can cause the cardiovascular collapse of your pet.

with enough room to move around without injuring itself. There are ventilation holes punched in the cardboard. Of course, if you intend to do a lot of cockatiel transporting, it would be useful to have a more substantial traveling cage. You can make such a cage yourself from wood. The ideal size is about 12 by 10 by 10 inches (30 × 25 × 25 cm), with a fine, wire-mesh front. Whatever kind of traveling cage you use, ensure that the ventilation holes are not blocked by labels, wrapping material, or such.

Sufficient seed for the journey may be strewn on the bottom of the traveling case, and if your journey is a long one, a little moist bread will supply the necessary moisture. Do not be concerned that the bird will be unable to find the seed in the dark confines of the cage. During various study trips to Australia, I regularly observed cockatiels, budgerigars, rosellas, cockatoos, and other birds foraging for food in the evenings and even at night by weak moonlight. I have also regularly seen my aviary birds feeding late into dusk. Thus, it is possible to transport cockatiels comfortably and safely, even over longer distances, as long as the trip does not exceed four hours.

Installing the Bird in Its New Home

When you arrive at home with your new pet, first ensure that all doors, windows, and similar openings are secure, that there are no unguarded open fires, and that all gas or electric appliances are switched off. Once all is in order, you can transfer the bird from its traveling case to its permanent cage. The best method of doing this is to place the open doors of the case and the cage together; generally, after a little hesitation, the bird will move to its new home.

It is advisable to install a bird in its new cage as early in the day as possible, preferably before noon, so that it has ample time to settle into these strange surroundings before nightfall. It will also give your new bird time to get to know the positions of the various perches and to choose the one it will use to roost at night. If you place a bird in a new cage late in the afternoon or evening, there is a chance that it will remain restless, fluttering about all night and possibly hurting itself.

Many newly purchased birds spend their early days in a large aviary or flight, often with many other birds. Others may come from the well-known barred parrot cages, and thus will already be accustomed to seed and water containers. After introducing your bird to its new cage, keep a close eye—from a distance—and ensure that it quickly finds its food dish. In case of doubt, scatter some seed on the floor of the cage. Cockatiels are natural ground feeders, so they will not starve as long as there is a supply of seed on the floor. Although a seed container might be right "in front of the bird's nose," as it were, a cockatiel unac-

A pearl pied cockatiel and its friend. This is a very interesting color mutation as it is sex-linked (pearl) and recessive or autosomal (pied).

quainted with that particular type of food hopper may take a while to figure out exactly what it is and what is in it. Moreover, after a long, stressful, and tiring journey, your bird will

Hand-tamed white face white cockatiel; see also photos of this mutation on pages 149 and 157.

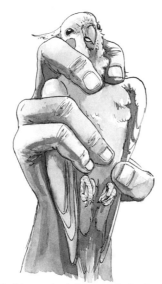

To hold a cockatiel correctly, its head should be positioned between the first two fingers. Do not grip too tightly on the neck and upper breast as this could compress the windpipe. Leather gloves may be necessary, especially with new birds.

want to find its food with a minimum amount of hassle. After a few days, it will have discovered the benefits of the food hopper, and it will then be no longer necessary for you to strew seed on the floor.

Handling Your New Pet

As a rule, newly arrived cockatiels should be handled as little as possible. They certainly don't like being gripped, and can easily be shocked. But sometimes it may be necessary to catch a bird and remove it from its cage. Catching a bird can have bad consequences. If one is too rough, there is a chance that the bird will be injured. If one is too slow, the catching process will take too long and the bird will become tired out. It is easiest to catch a cockatiel when it is in a small cage. First place your gloved hand in the cage, wait a few seconds for the bird to calm down, then, moving quickly and carefully, grab the whole bird in your hand.

In a larger cage or aviary, it will be necessary to use a net with a diameter of about 14 inches (35 cm) and a depth of about 20 inches (50 cm). Such nets can be purchased from your avicultural suppliers, or you can make one yourself from a piece of strong, net curtain material. The handle should be about 20 inches (50 cm) long, perhaps longer for extra large or tall aviaries.

In general, use the net to catch a bird while it is in flight, thus decreasing the possibility of injury. This possibility can be further decreased by fitting some foam rubber around the hard rim of the net. The bird must be caught quickly and cleanly; do not allow the process to develop into a wild hunt, which will be very distressing and possibly injurious to the bird.

If a number of birds are to be caught from an aviary, you should take them in two or three attempts. Better to spend two five-minute catching periods than one ten-minute marathon. A shorter catching time is not so exhausting for the birds. Occasionally, breeders who take too long catching birds will find a number of dead birds on their hands. One must be very careful in dealing with cockatiels.

The First Few Weeks

As a general guide for the new bird owner, here are some words of advice about the first few weeks.

• On arrival, have your birds immediately examined by an experienced fancier or an avian veterinarian.

• Quarantine new birds by keeping them isolated from existing stock for at least two weeks, in a totally separate room, in order to avoid bringing infectious diseases into your stock.

• Allow your new cockatiels time to relax. Put them in a place where they will not be bothered by loud noises and harassment from other animals, like barking dogs. Leave the birds alone as much as possible. Do not show them off to all your friends and acquaintances. Wait for this "coming out" party until the birds have become completely accustomed to their cage or room aviary and are comfortable among people; avoid excessive handling at all times.

• House the cockatiels in a rectangular cage, not a round one, which makes the birds nervous. The cage should be as large as possible (see page 19), with the perches arranged so that ruffling of the tail feathers can be avoided. Place the cage at eye level in a corner; this gives the birds a sense of safety and security.

• Maintain a stable temperature of approximately 80°F (27°C) during the first 25–30 days. Use a heat lamp or, better still, an infrared lamp; avoid all sorts of portable heaters

This male cockatiel just arrived in its new home—so everything is still strange. Nevertheless, it is a good idea to introduce the new bird to your hand, especially if you want to make it your pet. A bird should be allowed some 10 to 12 days to get fully accustomed to its new surroundings before any serious training is started.

It is advisable that one person in the household undertakes the training in the beginning to help prevent the bird from becoming confused by different voices and manners.

17

It is also advisable to visit your avian veterinarian shortly after you have purchased a new bird, so he or she can examine the animal and start a medical record. The doctor will usually ask you to bring samples of fresh stools.

a high-protein stress-formula diet that is palatable. Diets that contain *Lactobacillus* predigested proteins (an easily metabolized source of quick energy) are preferable. Never change diets abruptly; do so gradually over a period of two to three weeks. Abrupt dietary changes often cause intestinal problems that can become extremely dangerous.

• Do not provide sand and/or grit for at least 10–15 days, as stress conditions and anxiety trigger overeating. This could cause dangerous health problems. Maintain proper hygiene, however.

• Cockatiels with extremely nervous behavior—often with almost constant wing flapping—must have their wings clipped in order to prevent serious bodily injury.

• Avoid placing the birds in total darkness at night; provide a small night light so each bird is able to find its perch, water, and food at all times. Give the bird at least 10–12 hours of total rest. Don't forget to provide fresh food and drinking water for the night.

• Avoid insecticides, paint fumes, smoke, open windows, long and direct sunlight (sunstroke), moldy seeds, unwashed vegetables and fruits, and spoiled drinking water (use spring water at room temperature).

because of the fire risk. After approximately 30 days, lower the heat to room temperature very gradually, over a period of 15–20 days.

• Avoid drafts, but maintain proper ventilation. Ideally, use a box cage, which is an opaque box constructed of thin metal or wood, with closed back and sides and an open front. This type of box eliminates the danger of drafts and also gives the birds a sense of security.

• Besides providing the food the birds are accustomed to, for four days (and only four days) feed them

Chapter Two

Housing, Care, and Management

Cockatiels and their various mutations are virtually domesticated birds that are not particularly fussy with regard to their housing. This does not mean, however, that their keepers should be satisfied with any little cage or makeshift aviary. We must all bear in mind the fact that our feathered friends are totally dependent upon us for their welfare. It is only with good and responsible husbandry that our birds will live long, healthy lives and, if we desire, reward us by enlarging their families.

Cages

There are many kinds of cages available commercially. By browsing around the pet shops, you will be able to examine a variety of these products, most of which are manufactured with the welfare of the birds in mind. There are, of course, unsuitable cages on the market, many of which are attractive to look at, but not fit for birds to live in. Personally, I prefer to allow each bird as much

freedom of movement as possible, though this of course does not mean that every decorative cage should be rejected arbitrarily. Tall tower models, for example, are unsuitable for cockatiels and at best are adequate only for a couple of small tropical finches or perhaps a pair of loving budgerigars. Cages with vertical bars should be reserved for canaries and other nonclimbing species. In general, the roomy, sometimes fancy cages with horizontal bars are suitable for cockatiels. For obvious reasons, we can never be sure of breeding success whatever cage we have, but those people wishing to keep a single pet bird are not worried about this aspect in any case; they want only a pet bird/companion to help create a cozy, companionable atmosphere in the home and, incidentally, to serve as an instant conversational topic when visitors arrive. It is the goal of this handbook to serve the needs of these fanciers as well as the needs of breeders and all other owners of cockatiels. I want to make them all aware of the actions they can take to keep their birds in

A variety of toys is always welcome. If you just purchased a bird from a fancier, shop, or breeder, it is possible that the bird is already fond of certain foods, treats, and toys. Ask if you could have some of the bird's "old toys" so it has something that is familiar to it in its new surrounding.

good health and in comfortable, nurturing surroundings.

Because cage designs frequently change (often for the better), I am purposely not going to provide a detailed description of the many models that may be available on the market. Fortunately, it has been many years since bird fanciers placed their birds in tiny, dark cages barely large enough for them to turn

Once tame, your bird will come to you and perch on your arm or hand when it is time for it to go back in its cage.

around, let alone exercise their wings. Currently available cages are usually not only roomy but also beautiful to look at, often finished in chrome or brass and with colorful bottoms made from hygienic plastic or Plexiglas®. These materials do not rust, a condition that is not only unsightly but also provides an excellent hiding place for disease organisms. Modern cage bottoms are also designed to prevent excess seed, husks, and droppings from falling to the floor. As the cage base is usually easy to separate from the top by undoing a few little clamps or by sliding it out, it is no longer necessary to catch the bird in order to clean its cage. Both birdcage and caged bird can be placed on a sheet of newspaper while the cage base can be cleaned in a matter of minutes. As most cages are equipped with one or more access doors, it is easy to remove the perches one at a time for cleaning and occasional sanding. The food and water containers are usually affixed to the cage in such a way that they can be removed, cleaned, and refilled with minimum disturbance to the birds.

Some cages may be suspended from special stands, and there are a number of attractive designs available. However, I am personally not in favor of these and would advise against buying one. Most cages on stands start to swing with the least amount of movement, and birds are not particularly fond of having their home turned into something resembling an amusement park ride. Cages

Hand-made wooden perches or dowels for cockatiels should have a diameter of ¾ inch. The perch is right when the bird's toes don't go all the way around it. Never, ever use sandpaper perch covers!

Cockatiels don't fly as much and as frequently as many other Australian parakeets in captivity; they must nevertheless have a reasonable amount of room for exercises. Remember this "rule" while constructing your own cages.

This white face pied cockatiel is inspecting its new manzanita perch. This kind of wood will be very hard to chew on.

should be placed on a solid, flat surface at as high a level as is practical; a good rule of thumb is that a bird should be able to look down on us, in a manner of speaking.

Currently, there are on the market "French cages," usually antiqued white with a pointed roof, curlicues, and what have you. It may be difficult to see the bird, but as long as there is room enough, I can see no strong objection to these cages. As far as the size of any cage is concerned,

the actual measurements should not be less than 39½ by 23½ by 23½ (100 × 60 × 60 cm) for a pair of birds, or 19½ by 17½ by 17½ inches (50 × 45 × 45 cm) for a single bird.

Accessories

Perches: Perches should be fashioned from good hardwood and should not be too thin. A diameter of half an inch (1.3 cm) will allow the bird to grasp the perch comfortably. A perch that is too thin can cause

Don't forget to replace the toys in the playpen regularly. Birds are very inquisitive and become bored when they always have to play with the same models. Obviously, you should keep toys and playpen spick and span clean!

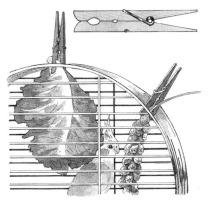

Clothespins can be very useful; they can hold greens and millet sprays, among other possibilities.

the bird a great deal of discomfort and necessitate frequent nail clipping. Rapid nail growth will result if the perch is too smooth and not flat enough along the top. A weekly scoring of the perches with a wire bristle perch scraper (sold in pet shops), an abrasive brush, a knife blade, or a rough file will get rid of excessive smoothness. Soak them in hot water with a chlorine bleach disinfecting solution, and let them dry in the sun (or otherwise) for 20 minutes before returning them to the cage. Perches are best placed in front of the seed and water hoppers, and one or two should be placed toward the top of the cage, with enough clearance so that the bird will not bump its head. It is very important to provide a high perch because cockatiels, like most birds, prefer to roost (sleep) as high up as possible. Never place so many perches in the cage that they interfere with the bird's flight and mobility. And one perch should never be placed directly above another; the droppings from the upper perch will soil the lower perch or will soil the plumage of the bird beneath (if there is more than one bird in the cage). A slight variation in perch thicknesses will help exercise the bird's feet, relax its muscles, and keep its toenails worn to a reasonable length.

Toys: Birds require various forms of entertainment and social activity. For cockatiels that have to spend many hours alone, toys are especially valuable because they keep them busy and prevent boredom.

This is important because bored cockatiels will start screaming, might pluck their own feathers, or might begin some other unpleasant habit.

Fortunately, a wide variety of toys is available. There are bells, swings, ladders, chains, ropes, etc., and all are very useful. Ensure that chain links are large enough to avoid accidents, such as catching the bird's toes.

I have noticed that many cockatiels are fascinated with a little key ring (and keys!) or a small metal spoon. Mirrors and other shiny objects—and many of these are on the market—are appreciated. Be certain, however, that the birds cannot break the mirror.

Certain rubber and soft plastic toys can be dangerous. According to R. Dean Axelson, DVM: "Rubber is acted upon by the digestive enzymes, releasing toxins that damage the bowel lining and paralyze

That's a tough one!

the intestinal muscles. The result can be blockage of the bowel and death, so make a point of keeping rubber toys away from your pet."

Nest inspection. It sometimes takes a couple of days before the female decides to take or to reject the offered nest box. It is therefore advisable to offer various nest boxes, different in size and shape.

Ideal recreational items for birds include toys and blocks of hardwood, seashells, and rawhide (rings, etc.). Other good choices include fresh bark-covered tree branches, raw vegetables (carrots and potatoes), banana skins, dried gourds, coconut shells, etc.

A cockatiel will not necessarily accept all toys right away; it can take several days (or even weeks!) before the bird will begin to play with them. Any toys given to cockatiels must be cleaned and sterilized at regular intervals.

Fancy Clothespins: The fancy clothespins that are used for holding memos and letters can also be useful to the bird fancier. About 6 inches (15 cm) long and made of wood (do not use the plastic variety), they can keep a cage door open or serve as a clamp for holding greens, seeding weed stalks, millet sprays, or strips of carrot. They can even serve as perches, with the added advantage that these little resting places can be added or moved practically anywhere in the cage. In the aviary, too, fancy clothespins have their uses, such as clamping greens and seed stalks to the wire or between the nesting boxes. No doubt there are many more possibilities that you will be able to discover for yourself.

Breeding Cages

Various types of commercially available cages have been designed especially for breeding birds. These are usually constructed of solid metal, wood, or plastic on the roof, floor, back, and ends. Only the front is open (open fronted), and this is covered with a grille of mesh or trellis.

Cockatiels feel safer in breeding cages than they do in all-wire cages, and they have a greater protection from cold and drafts. The breeding cage should be placed securely in a well-lit location, preferably where unfiltered sunlight can be made available.

A breeding cage should be about 39 to 48 inches long, 38 to 40 inches deep, and 24 to 28 inches high (99–122 × 96–102 × 61–71 cm). Some commercially available models are constructed in such a way that they can be stacked next to, or on top of, each other. This is very convenient in a birdroom where lim-

Breeding cages are available in a variety of sizes. Stay away from locations that are directly in front of a window to avoid direct sunlight during the greater part of the day, and flashing, disturbing lights during the evening and night.

ited space is available. Other types of cages may have removable sides, making it easy to join cages together. Look over the various possibilities at a bird show or at your local suppliers.

Many hobbyists prefer to construct their own breeding cages. Not only does this usually save money, but it also enables fanciers to design cages exactly to their own requirements. Front grilles are available commercially. In most instances, the largest sizes should be selected and the cages built to accommodate them. If the grille fronts available are not big enough, it is fairly easy to mount several of them in a frame that fits snugly into the main body of the cage. Leave a space at the bottom of the frame so that you can slide a removable tray in and out, making cleaning chores that much easier. If you are constructing a battery of cages, be sure that the fronts have enough doors and openings to allow convenient servicing. It is best to use food and water dishes that can be serviced from outside the cage. In addition, nest boxes can be fitted to the outside of the cage front or end, so that health and safety checks can be carried out without undue disturbance to the birds.

Box Cages

Most birds feel safer and more comfortable in a cage that offers them a certain amount of privacy. A cage that is closed in on most sides offers a good environment for most birds. The box cage, which is closed

Part of the author's aviaries.

on three sides and which has bars only in the front, is probably the most suitable type of cage (see also Breeding Cages, page 24). Such a cage should measure not less than 10 inches wide by 15 inches long by 18 inches high (25 × 38 × 46 cm). Box cages must be situated so that they receive adequate, but not excessive, light. If such a cage were situated so that it received the full impact of the sun for a good part of the day, the birds would soon be "cooked."

Box cages of the recommended dimensions are also ideally suited for breeding pairs because they offer so much privacy to birds brooding and rearing their offspring. We have already discussed the breeding cage, which is a variation of the box cage.

The Aviary

Before discussing aviaries and their construction, I should point out that cockatiels are certainly not out of place in the community aviary. They are probably the least aggressive of the parrot-like birds and will coexist relatively peaceably with other cockatiels or even other exotic birds as long as the living area is of sufficient size (see page 29). This does not mean that cockatiels never fight a round or two. When two cocks are kept in the same cage, there will be occasional acts of aggression. On the other hand, when three males are placed together, there will be no disagreements at all. They will share their lives together in peace and harmony, since their basically innocent pursuits and seemingly threatening gestures do not mean anything.

On the other hand, you should ensure that other bird species in the aviary do not terrorize your cockatiels. As a general rule, only birds smaller than, or of the same size as,

Cockatiels can live with various finches and other seed-eating birds in a large aviary without the risk of massacres, as long as other parrot-like birds are not included. Note the container drawer, which can be pushed inside the aviary when filled with treats or daily seed mixtures.

your cockatiels should be placed in the same aviary. I once kept a male red-rumped parrot *(Psephotus haematonotus)* with cockatiels, and it turned out to be a proper little bully toward certain male cockatiels, literally mopping the floor with them! All this terrorizing took place on the second day that he was in the aviary. Always keep an alert eye on your birds so that any hostile attitudes can be detected before it is too late. You should be particularly watchful when placing new birds into the aviary.

Many aviculturists are totally against placing budgerigars or any other hook-beaked species in an aviary with cockatiels, and rightly so. It is not unusual for parakeets to aim for each other's toes in their acts of aggression, and they will do the same with cockatiels. Although our hook-beaked friends will adequately defend themselves from each other, cockatiels are quite timid in this respect with other psittacines, and wounded feet and toes result from this type of communal living. In addition, it is not wise to place many other birds with cockatiels that you wish to breed; like most birds, cockatiels like peace and quiet during the breeding season.

Cockatiels can be quite fussy in one area—perches. Cockatiels prefer sitting as high up as possible. It is thus important to place a number of perches in elevated locations, to avoid evening quarrels among cockatiels choosing their spot for the night. These perches should all be placed at the same height and close to the wall. It is unlikely that the settling-down proceedings will ever be completely peaceful, but this should eliminate most of the problems! I would point out once again that none of the perches should be placed in such a manner that a bird sitting on one will soil a bird sitting below. Allow for a variety in the thickness of perches, ranging from ½ to 1 inch (1.3–2.6 cm) in diameter (see page 21). Natural wood (willow, manzanita) gives different diameters and is, therefore, very much recommended for aviary and cage (see page 21).

To avoid feeding quarrels, place several water and seed containers in the aviary. Nothing is as important in the community aviary as peace and tolerance. If these elements are not present, there is little or no chance of achieving good breeding results.

A community aviary should be equipped with more than enough nest boxes, preferably twice as many nesting facilities as there are pairs of birds. Do not hang the nest boxes too close together, again to avoid arguments; allow at least 4 feet (1.2 m) between the boxes.

There are several types of accommodations suitable for keeping cockatiels that you want to breed. If you are not intent on producing prime examples of particular color varieties, and are not particular about the various color factors, you can house a number of different cockatiels in an aviary, possibly with a few other peaceable species. But

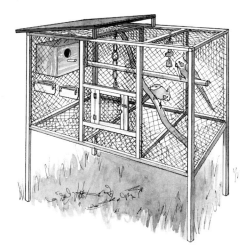

The Noegel aviary is very sanitary as it has a mesh bottom through which droppings and uneaten food can pass. This small aviary, with its night shelter box, is suitable for a pair of birds in an area that has mild winters.

if you want to breed a particular color variety, you should keep only homozygous or true-breeding birds (see page 148). In this way you will know exactly what colors will be

A simple but adequate garden aviary.

A group aviary—and what a beautiful group it is!

passed on to successive generations. If you place a random collection of birds together, you will get a potpourri of colors and combinations of colors in any offspring.

If you plan and maintain an aviary wisely, it can be an ideal housing facility for cockatiels. Of course, first-class breeders who want to breed more than one color variety will find it necessary to build more aviaries. Each aviary will then be used to produce just one particular color mutation. The aviaries need not be excessively large, but there should be sufficient room to allow adequate freedom of movement for the inhabitants. The following notes should help the do-it-yourselfer build an ideal aviary, adapted to his or her own specific requirements.

Materials

Wood alone should not be used in an aviary designed for cockatiels.

Sooner or later the structure is likely to be visited by mice, rats, weasels, or some neighborhood cats. It is obviously important to build an aviary to exclude these pests. The foundation should be concrete and the framework made of 2- by 4-inch (5- × 10-cm) timber studs strengthened with metal stripping. On top of the foundation, build a wall about 12 to 15 inches (30–40 cm) high. Build the floor at that same height, again preferably from concrete, particularly in the night shelters, though kiln-dried or creosote-treated planks can also be used; tile, too, can be useful here. For the outer walls and even the inner dividing panels, your best choice is exterior plywood. Although a further covering is not necessary, the roof will look very attractive if it is finished with roofing tiles or slate. The roof should slope at a shallow angle. If the aviary is built against an existing fence or wall, the roof should extend just a little to avoid water collecting where it is connected to the fence; a strip of asphalt or tar paper can do a lot to eliminate this problem as well. Apart from the materials mentioned above, you will need sturdy wire mesh (1 by ½ inch [2.5 × 1.3 cm] 19 gauge galvanized twilled or weldmesh), wire strands, nails, and glass. A plastic or aluminum gutter is also very useful.

Shape and Size

With an aviary, first you determine what size aviary can be built in the space and location available, and from that the number of birds. If you have ample space, you can try to keep and breed birds on a community basis (several males and several females) but with birds of the same color in order to maintain pure (homozygous) birds.

In deciding on the shape of the aviary, I recommend that you try not to be overambitious. Stick to conventional straight lines, at least to the extent that the aviary will fit into its surroundings. The focal point of the aviary should be your birds, so various means of embellishing the aviary's exterior, such as little domes and towers, are generally not a good idea. An aviary that blends in with nature by the addition of all kinds of flowers and shrubs is usually much more attractive. An aviary should never be too low; the minimum height should be approximately 8 feet (about 2.5 m).

An ideal aviary is divided into three parts: a completely enclosed night shelter, an open flight, and a partially covered flight. The night shelter offers protection against bad weather conditions, provides shade during hot, sunny weather, and allows the birds to rest peaceably. It could be eliminated in areas with mild winters as long as part of the flight is well protected. Nest boxes are best placed in the protected part. Personally, I have found that most cockatiels prefer to breed in the night shelter, providing it is well-lit. This can be readily achieved by having a window installed in one of the walls. In summer the window can be opened to provide fresh air

as long as this does not create a draft. A completely free-standing aviary (not one that is built against an existing fence or garage) can be built with the nest boxes affixed against the back wall on specially installed wooden slats.

Many fanciers in warmer areas such as Florida and southern California prefer completely open aviaries, and these certainly seem to promote the desire to breed. These aviaries have two parts, one open, one covered, with a few large, half-open breeding boxes or specially made night shelter boxes substituting for the night shelter. A typical night shelter box measures 23.5 to 31.5 inches (60–80 cm) long and 12 inches (30 cm) high, and consists of two end walls, a back wall, and a roof. You can install a few perches in these shelter boxes, provided, as mentioned, that they are not situated directly over one another.

If you have the time and, especially, the money . . . .

The Closed Area or Night Shelter

A tiny "entrance" hall or safety porch with double doors is built in front of the night shelter so that birds do not escape when someone enters or leaves the aviary. Once in this little porch, a visitor naturally closes the outer door before opening the inner one and entering the night shelter. This inner area is divided in half horizontally. The top half is actually the night shelter. The bottom half is divided in two vertically. One side is used as a pairing room, quarantine station, confine-

A beautiful pied cockatiel resting on a manzanita perch. These perches come in various lengths and diameters. They are ideal in the night shelter of an aviary where they can be placed horizontally.

ment area for troublemakers, observation room, etc.; the other side is used as a storage space for nesting boxes, perches, water and seed dishes, and other equipment. The floors of both bottom and top halves should be made of concrete or tile, though the floor of the night shelter should be covered with a 3-inch (6–8-cm) layer of sand and grit. The sides of the night shelter are made of wire mesh.

It is highly recommended that the night shelter be built in such a way that the birds can be easily shut in. There are always birds that want to get out once they have been persuaded to go in. The pop-hole through which the birds gain entry to and exit from the night shelter should have a sliding door (mounted in a couple of aluminum strips) that can be controlled, preferably from the outside of the aviary, with a nylon rope or a metal rod. (Any part of the rope that is inside the aviary should be run through a metal pipe or the birds will chew it.) The little door should be reasonably heavy (a piece of plywood covered with aluminum sheeting will close easily and—thanks to the metal jacket— will not be subject to gnawing by the birds).

As has been stated, most birds, including cockatiels, like to spend their nights in as high a position as possible. By making the night shelter higher than the outside flight you encourage your birds to use it. Any birds that remain reluctant to use the night shelter should be locked in for two to three weeks. When they get used to the shelter, they can be given access to the outside flight.

Cockatiels are naturally most active during the mornings and evenings as they must fill their stomachs after and before darkness. During the middle of the day they are usually resting. This stems from the wild cockatiels' Australian habitat, where it would be dangerous to expend too much energy during the heat of the afternoon. In fact, many cockatiels sit inside the night shelter during the day. As mentioned, you should ensure that the shelter is not drafty as cockatiels are sensitive to drafts.

On cold, wintry days the birds can be kept permanently locked in the shelter. Although cockatiels are surprisingly hardy, it is better to be safe than sorry. A closed shelter will protect the birds from chilling winds and be slightly warmer than the outside flight. Although the shelter need not be as large as the flight, take into consideration that the birds may have to be locked in during a severe winter and allow them some freedom of movement. Flying around helps the birds keep warm. Temperatures in the night shelters should not fall below freezing. During times when this is likely to occur, move the birds indoors—perhaps into an attic room, where indoor flights can be constructed.

Supplementary Heating and Lighting: The provision of additional heating should also be considered. Most bird fanciers maintain that cockatiels require no supplementary heating in most temperate winters, but we really cannot expect them to thrive in temperatures of 20°F (–4°C) or worse. Moreover, it is not very comfortable for fanciers to tend their birds in such extreme cold. A little heating will prevent the drinking water from freezing and will also help prevent disease by drying out the air in the shelter. Every fancier with some experience knows that the incidence of sickness increases during the colder, damper parts of the year. Low temperatures and moisture combined will lower the birds' resistance to pathogens. Positive advantages can therefore be expected if your birds are protected from biting winds, fog, drizzles, and downpours.

A playpen as part of the aviary pictured on page 5.

In an open flight there is always room for a birdbath or a little, shallow pool, as cockatiels (and all other birds for that matter) love to take a bath. The flagstones around the pool keep the birds' nails short. How is that for a beauty treatment? This lutino is going to find out.

than a few degrees above freezing; otherwise the difference between the inner and outer temperatures will be too great and will cause the birds to lose their normal resistance, especially if they are passing through the molt.

Feed hoppers are usually placed inside the shelter where they will be protected from the elements; the birds will be able to feed in comfort, and the fancier will be able to do the chores in cozier surroundings.

It is recommended that supplementary lighting also be included in the night shelters. One or two broad spectrum fluorescents in the service corridor will provide sufficient light for all of the compartments. You should ensure that electric cables do not pass through the individual shelters, where the birds could reach them and gnaw at them; otherwise, disasters will be guaranteed!

Access: With large numbers of aviaries, a corridor along the rear of the shelters is a must; such an arrangement leads to efficiency and time-saving in the care of your birds. An ideal situation is to make the enclosed shelter wide enough to have a central corridor with the night shelter on the flight side and room— 20–24 inches (50–60 cm)—for a number of cages on the other.

The entrance doors to the night shelters should be relatively narrow and have low headroom, so that birds cannot easily escape when you open the door. Another method of reducing escapes is to have a little feeding hatch in the side of

Any of the conventional heat sources may be considered. However, kerosene heating can be unhealthy and electrical heating can be very expensive. Gas heating is good, but the best solution is to have the aviary hooked into your central heating system. In fact, before building an aviary, you must think about supplying water, electricity, and heat, and decide whether to include them in your basic plan. For instance, it is convenient to have a water tap installed in the shelter. It can be used during cleaning chores and also for the drinking water supply. It can be very expensive to make alterations later.

Heating apparatus should not bring the internal temperatures more

each shelter, so that you do not have to enter at routine feeding and watering time; the larger entrance door is then used only for other activities such as cleaning, installing and removing nest boxes, catching birds, and so on.

The individual night shelters are usually separated from each other and from the service corridor by wire mesh. Although the birds can see each other, I have not experienced many problems; and pairs in adjoining compartments soon get accustomed to each other. Moreover, if rare problems of aggressiveness between individual birds should occur, you can move the combatants to nonadjoining compartments. An advantage of the wire mesh is that the birds are all able to see you as you enter the service corridor; in enclosed compartments, they only hear your entrance, don't know what is causing the noise, and may become nervous.

The Open Area or Flight

The completely open part of the aviary serves to toughen up birds and keep them in "good color"; furthermore, it gives them a feeling of freedom, which can only enhance their desire to breed. The entire flight can be constructed from treated 2- by 4-inch (5- × 10-cm) timber or iron poles, with the walls and roof made of wire mesh. It is preferable to have a dirt floor in this area, so that some plants and bushes can be planted. After the perches have been properly installed, the birds will have plenty of resting and pairing places and can unrestrictedly enjoy the sun and the occasional shower.

It is adequate and convenient to make the aviary and night shelter 36 inches (approximately 1 meter) in width, as most wire meshes are available in this size. You should bear this in mind when planning and building aviaries; it will save you a lot of cutting and clipping. New wire has the disadvantage of glistening in the light, which makes it difficult to observe the contents of the aviary. You can overcome this by applying a nontoxic, black matte paint to the wire with a roller (needless to say, the paint must be thoroughly dry before the birds are introduced).

Lumber is mainly used for the construction of the framework as it is relatively inexpensive and easy to cut, and the wire is easy to attach to it. A disadvantage of wood is that parakeets (although cockatiels are not as bad as some other species) will gnaw into it, soon destroying the framework if unchecked. Methods of preventing gnawing of the framework include attaching the wire to the *inside* of the framework or covering the parts of the framework accessible to the birds with sheet metal (aluminum or galvanized steel).

Another possibility, of course, is to use metal poles. They may be more expensive, they can be slightly less attractive, and it is more difficult to attach the wire mesh, but such poles will last much longer and will not be gnawed by the birds.

If you have several aviaries, there are several ways you can plan your access. If you build a corridor along the narrower ends of the flights, the birds are less likely to be disturbed by comings and goings. However, if you want to save expense, it is possible to have doors leading from one flight to the next. In this case, of course, you will lose space for affixing perches where the door swings open. The birds will also lose flying distance. You can overcome this problem to some extent by limiting the height of the doors so that there are perch spaces above them, but this may further hinder your comfortable access. The doors are thus best placed in the center of the flights. Secure door latches are essential, as cockatiels are curious by nature and can soon learn to open insecure latches.

Drinking receptacles are best placed toward the front end of the flights, where they can be easily filled with a hose or watering can. It is highly recommended that there be a secure, sliding hatch in the wall of the flights so that you can clean the water receptacles without entering the aviary. Such water receptacles should obviously not be situated directly below perches.

Some fanciers like to cover the flight wholly or partly with a solid roof. This is said to decrease the possibility of worm infections from wild birds and also provides a certain amount of protection from the weather. A disadvantage, however, is that during the warmer months it can have the effect of producing an oven-like atmosphere. A partially covered flight gives the birds a choice, so that they are able to take shelter from strong sunlight or heavy rain. They will then have a choice of being inside, inside/outside, or outside!

It must also be taken into account that plastic, glass, and other transparent materials hinder the passage of ultraviolet rays and thus reduce the possibility of birds forming sufficient quantities of vitamin D.

Nest boxes may be erected in the outside flights if the roof is (partly) covered.

The Covered Area

This area should have a waterproof roof and perhaps a solid back wall separating it from the night shelter. The rest should be covered with wire mesh. A dirt floor is suitable, though one made of concrete slabs or solid concrete, covered with a generous layer of sand, is also excellent. With a concrete floor, of course, any small bushes or fresh willow and privet branches will have to be placed in tubs or other large planters and will need to be replaced as necessary.

This area will, of course, also need to be equipped with perches. Like those in the open flight, these perches must be cleaned regularly, though those outside are likely to be pretty well taken care of by the rain. Perhaps when you water the plants you could hose off the perches at the same time. In any event, they should be checked regularly.

General Remarks About Aviary Construction

• When making the foundation, ensure that the bottom edge of the wire mesh can be buried in the ground to help keep out mice and rats. Adding wire to a solid concrete floor during pouring will help prevent cracking.

• Be sure the roof covering extends over the edges of the aviary at all points.

• If you intend to keep other parrot-like birds such as lovebirds or budgerigars in adjoining flights, it is best to have double-wired partitions. Some of these hook-billed birds spend a lot of time clambering about on the wire, and they will think nothing of grabbing a cockatiel's toe or foot that happens to be sticking through the wire.

• Be sure to use only child-safe paint on any internal surfaces, as these paints do not contain lead or other potentially harmful ingredients. All paint must obviously be well dried before birds are introduced. Whitewashing is not a good idea because most whitewashes contain some harmful elements and sooner or later most will begin to peel. Pieces that are then picked up by the birds can be harmful to their health.

Maintenance

The sand you sprinkle on the aviary floor will need to be replaced regularly, and the soil will need to be turned on a regular basis, the frequency depending on the size of the aviary and the number of inhabitants. At least once a year, every spring for example, all perches, sleeping quarters, and any other little hiding places should be cleaned and disinfected. All shrubbery and any other natural perches for cockatiels must be pruned whenever necessary, any rotting or dying pieces removed from the aviary, and any dead plants should be replaced. All woodwork and metal in the aviary must be thoroughly hosed off and inspected.

If at all possible, during the cleaning of an aviary, the resident birds should be temporarily housed in flight cages, allowing you the opportunity to clean both the interior and the exterior thoroughly and to repair any leaks, drafty cracks, faults in the wire, locks, and so on—in short, to bring everything back to top form. Should you decide to keep your birds indoors for the winter—and you may include winter-hardened birds that could spend the winter outside—this would be the ideal period to check and repair everything at your leisure. If you repeat this procedure every year, it is most unlikely that you will be surprised by a great many problems at any one time. During the winter, when one does not breed birds anyway, be sure to do a thorough cleaning job on the nest boxes. These enclosures are favorite breeding grounds for bacteria, and diseases could easily develop a stronghold here. Apart from nest boxes you should also take care of feed hoppers, water dishes and fountains, birdbaths, and other accessories. The feed and water dishes should be placed in such a way that you have easy access to them without disturbing the birds too much.

Keep your aviary as clean as you can. Both you and your birds will benefit.

Unwelcome Visitors

In most cases the unwelcome guests will be mice or cats, the former after the birds' food, the latter after the birds themselves! There are other animal pests, too, including moles, rats, weasels, owls, and other birds of prey. In addition, we have the less noticeable pests such as bird lice.

One of the biggest problems for the aviary owner can be caused by mice. These little pests seem to be able to gain entry to every aviary at some time or another. Owing to their small size, mice can get through the smallest-gauge aviary mesh, and even the tiniest hole will allow them to get into the night shelter. Always build your aviary with mice in mind. Make everything as mouse-proof as possible. Ensure that there are no dark corners or accessible cavities, as mice show a preference for such areas. All internal areas of the aviary and shelter should be as light as possible. If you insulate the shelter or roof with cavity walls, don't give the mice any opportunity to enter the cavity and set up home. They will be extremely difficult to get rid of and will delight in destroying your insulation materials.

One method of controlling mice is to place dark, almost totally enclosed boxes with a little hay or straw inside. As there are no other dark places in the aviary, the mice are likely to nest in the boxes. After a few days, you can close the entrance, trapping the mice inside and then disposing of them humanely.

Cats can be a great problem in that they will scare the birds at night, causing them to panic and injure themselves. One of the best methods of keeping cats at bay is to use an electric wire. Apparatus is available from specialist suppliers. The type of electric fence used by farmers can also be used to good effect, and it may be possible to buy second-hand material at much reduced cost. An aviary may be double wired to prevent cats from reaching the birds, but you will still have the problem of preventing panic.

After a time, cats will realize that they cannot gain access to the birds and will then leave them alone. The situation also works in reverse, in that the birds will get used to a familiar cat and will not panic when they see it. However, if a strange cat should arrive on the scene, total bedlam will ensue.

Moles do no direct harm to the birds, but they undermine the aviary structure and also make entrance easier for other vermin. Rats and weasels usually gain access to an aviary with shallow foundations or no foundations at all. Rats can cause enormous structural damage to the aviary as well as attack the

The majority of healthy, fully mature cockatiels are ready to start breeding in the spring, regardless of whether they are housed in a garden aviary outdoors or indoors in a bird room. Cockatiels often don't mind if the nest box is a little smaller than the one shown on pages 21 and 23, and design details are really not important.

birds and their nests. They also pollute the food. Even a single weasel or stoat in the aviary will create untold havoc. Since it is important to exclude such pests, aviaries must then be constructed with every bit of ingenuity and craft you can muster. Otherwise, you may have only yourself to blame should a disaster occur.

Birds of prey can sit on top of the aviary or make mock attacks at the birds inside, causing panic and, possibly, injuries. Owls are said to be kept at bay by placing white, glazed balls on the aviary roof at night.

The Bird Room

A bird room is really little more than an outside aviary erected indoors or in an enclosed porch. The construction is basically the same, using wire mesh for the windows and the little entrance hall or safety porch.

Breeders of color mutations are greatly in favor of using a bird room, which is also an excellent place to keep tropical and subtropical birds. I am thinking here, of course, of the possibility of keeping a few rarer species together with cockatiels, provided the birds are compatible. In particular, expensive birds such as some of the larger tropical softbills and various Australian grass finches are really much better off in such a facility.

Quite often, a bird room will be found to be even more efficient and appropriate than an outside aviary, especially for those who are able to use one room in their home just for this hobby. It goes without saying that some prior planning will do much to make a bird room efficient and enjoyable. The best floor for a bird room is made of tiles (quarry tiles, of the type used on laundry floors, are excellent), covered with a layer of sand that must be replaced regularly. For aesthetic purposes, the bird room may be enhanced with a number of shrubs and trees placed in tubs and large pots. If you keep a spare set of plants and tubs, you can change them over at regular intervals, allowing those that have been ravaged and soiled by the birds to have a regular period of "rest and recuperation." A little insight can help recreate a lovely piece of nature right inside the home!

Location of Cages and Aviaries

Cages (with a pair of cockatiels, for example) and aviaries (with perhaps a group of birds) both need plenty of light and direct sunshine. North-facing rooms are totally unsuitable, as are areas of the garden that face north. One should also think twice before installing a cage in one of those "ideal little corners," which are often dark. The broad spectrum lights that are available can be very helpful to bird keepers who cannot provide sufficient amounts of direct sunlight. Fluorescent or sun lamps as substitutes for natural sunlight will lead to trouble sooner or later (see page 31).

I do not mean to imply here that birds are unable to survive for a few days under these artificial conditions; certainly they could, but this is hardly the point. In my opinion, at least, keeping birds means keeping their health and beauty in peak condition. The plumage of birds that do not experience the benefit of natural sunlight will soon lose its color and luster. Such birds are slowly but inexorably reduced to pitiful heaps of feathers, pining away their lives. All too often I have seen lovely (and expensive) birds housed in such an unsatisfactory manner and slowly dying, although all other requirements were taken care of in the best possible way.

You can compare the care of birds with the care of house plants; no matter how excellent our care and knowledge of plants, if we deny them light—and in the case of many species, direct sunlight—they will soon lose their beauty and diminish into a stringy bunch of stalks doomed to disappear into the garbage can.

A major requirement, then, for a cage or aviary is that its front faces south (I am speaking here of the so-called box cage, in which only the front has bars). If this is not feasible, then face the front of the cage or aviary in as near a southerly direction as possible, preferably in a southeasterly rather than a southwesterly direction. Part of the aviary front should be made of glass, especially if the front does not face south. In addition to these requirements, the aviary should be built in a location that is both attractive and easy to observe, preferably surrounded with shrubs and flowers to enhance its aesthetic appeal.

Indoor aviaries, too, should have a southerly aspect if at all possible. As already stated, the same holds true for cages. Here, too, southeast is preferable to southwest, if south is not possible. The whole idea is that your birds will be better off if you position them so that they are able to enjoy the sunshine for a few hours every day. Suitable locations indoors will also be ideal places for indoor plants. With a little artistic imagination, you can arrange birds and plants in such a way that the whole setup will look pleasing and natural. Nothing can be more disturbing than seeing a bird cage located obviously out of place.

Location requirements can be summarized as follows:

• An aviary or cage facing north will receive little or no sunlight and will be subject to cold winds and driving rain.

• Facing east, the aviary will receive morning sunlight but little or no sun in the afternoon and evening. In summer the winds will be warm and dry, but winter winds will be stark and cold; there will be few, if any, driving rains.

• Facing south, the birds will receive sunlight from early morning to late in the evening, with driving rains and strong winds varying from place to place and season to season.

• Facing west, the aviary will receive sunlight in the afternoons and evenings; it will be subject to strong winds and sometimes driving rains, particularly in the fall.

Do not forget that the presence and arrangement of natural or cultivated plants will play an important part in the protection of your aviary, almost as important as the structure itself. Whether you live in the middle of town or out in the country will also affect the degree of protection you will have to provide for your birds.

Remember, too, that prolonged periods of sunlight can overheat the interior of the aviary shelter so that the birds will then be reluctant to enter it. If any nest boxes are located in the shelter, your breeding results will be poor unless you provide for adequate ventilation. Mesh-protected windows that can be opened and closed as necessary are desirable.

I would like to mention two more points with regard to location. First, an aviary should be situated so that it can be seen easily from the house. Second, an aviary should not be situated where the birds will be subjected to noise, passing car lights, and similar disturbances. It is important that the birds be able to rest easily at night. Fortunately, birds are able to adapt to most such situations, especially if they are regular; but it's best to plan so as to avoid potential problems.

Aviculturists will ultimately find their own procedures for dealing with various situations, within their own financial constraints.

Before you begin to build an aviary, try to visit as many other fanciers as possible to see what they have built and to find out what problems, if any, they have experienced. Do not be afraid to ask for an explanation of anything that is not completely clear to you. And do not omit the most important question:

Plants for an outdoor aviary. Top: Douglas fir; right: English holly; bottom left: climbing rose; bottom right: English hawthorn.

• *What would you alter if you were to build again?*

One can often learn more from negative than from positive experiences!

Plantings

Many outside aviaries and other types of housing are poorly landscaped, with few if any trees and shrubs. It is often assumed, quite incorrectly, that it will be sufficient to supply cockatiels with a number of artificial perches. It should be borne in mind, however, that these birds like to spend a lot of time outside in the sunshine, though not necessarily in the direct rays of the sun. There is really no better way to help your birds fulfill their desire than by supplying ample shrubbery in an outdoor aviary, but without interfering with the flying space. An arrangement of plants and bushes will also stimulate birds to breed as such natural cover gives them a sense of protection and privacy. Evergreens are highly recommended, and they do not need to be all that expensive. One can usually find some bargains by inquiring about some of the "out-of-shape" bushes at the nursery. It's a good idea to place a few attractive dead trees in the covered part of the aviary, in addition to the necessary artificial perches.

I realize, of course, that cockatiels, being natural nibblers and gnawers (but maybe not as bad as some other hookbilled species), are not likely to leave plants in prime condition. In fact, plantings may have to be renewed at regular intervals. However, given ample care and regular pruning, greenery will last much longer than you might think. Of course, if you are able to rescue the original plants before they are completely ruined, you will most likely be able to revive them by planting them in large tubs or in some quiet corner of the garden. The birds will be thankful for the shrubs, especially in the heat of summer and during the colder months.

The following is a brief listing of those trees and shrubs that I have found to be useful in the cockatiel aviary:

American Arborvitae (Thuja occidentalis). This tree is particularly suitable for growing as a hedge in the aviary, especially in a community aviary with tropical birds. The scallop-shaped leaves are arranged in a cross design. In the past, schoolgirls would place a twig from this tree inside a handkerchief to enjoy the pleasant scent that can be brought out by rubbing it a little. These twigs are dark green above and light green beneath. Growing to a height of 50 feet (approximately 15 m), the American arborvitae, as its name suggests, originated in North America, but it is now extensively cultivated in many parts of the world. Only young specimens are suitable for use in the aviary, unless they are kept severely pruned to hedge proportions.

Austrian Pine (Pinus nigra). This is often used as a decorative tree. The blackish green needles can grow as long as 6 inches (15 cm) and stand in pairs. The bud produces resin. Young specimens are particularly attractive.

Climbing Rose (Rosa multiflora). This climbing rose is very suitable for the aviary. The small leaves are oval in shape and clearly indented. The stem will creep horizontally or climb vertically as the environment allows. The saber-shaped thorns are arranged in pairs. This plant may be used as a hedge and is excellent for use inside or outside the aviary for shelter and decoration.

Common Boxwood (Buxus sempervirens). Originating in the Mediterranean region, this evergreen is an excellent choice for the aviary. The small, oval leaves (maximum size: ¾ inch [2 cm]) are dark green above, lighter below, and have a leathery texture. A box hedge about 3 feet (1 m) long will be useful in the aviary. Many tropical birds, particularly several weaver varieties, like to build their nests in such a hedge.

Common Juniper (Juniperus communis). This evergreen can grow to a height of 33 feet (10 m) or more. Junipers take on various attractive and often bizarre shapes and are generally a decorative addition to the landscape, be it woods, moor, or planted forest. The needles are arranged in small wreaths in groups of three. The tree is ideal for the aviary and will do well even in poor soil.

Common Privet (Ligustrum vulgare). This hardy species, which originated in southern Europe and Asia Minor, is now world-renowned as a hedging plant. The sturdy, lance-shaped leaves, which grow to about 2 inches (5 cm) in length, are an excellent food for cockatiels. This hardwood shrub offers an ideal shade shelter for birds during the hotter parts of the year and provides excellent nesting sites for some tropical birds. In April and May little white flowers bloom in small hanging bunches. The common privet is one of the most popular aviary plants, a fact easily understood when one considers its many favorable attributes.

Douglas Fir (Pseudotsuga taxifolia or P. menziesii). The needles of this fir tree form two rows and are about 1 inch (2–3 cm) in length. They are a lovely light green above, while the underside is grayish green. There are irregularly placed little resin knobs on the bark. This species can grow to an enormous size, as much as 300 feet (90 m) in height and up to 13 feet (4 m) in diameter. Naturally, only very young trees are suitable for the aviary. This tree originated in North America but is now grown in many parts of the world.

English Hawthorn (Crataegus monogyna). This is a deciduous shrub that sheds its leaves in the fall. However, it has a dense network of thorny branches in which many birds like to nest. The deeply indented leaves have three to seven lobes. The red, bullet-shaped berries, which appear in the fall and often persist into the winter, are much enjoyed by birds. The shrub has very few demands other than being in a sunny situation.

English Holly (Ilex aquifolium). This evergreen shrub can grow to a tree of some 23 feet (7 m) in height. The glossy, dark-green, oval leaves, which grow to a length of about 3 inches (7–8 cm), have scalloped edges and sharp spines. The plant is tolerant of heavy pruning and is often seen fashioned into various novel shapes. Male and female bushes should be planted close to each other so that the red berries, much loved by birds, are produced. The small flowers are attached to short stems. The holly does best in moist soil in full sun.

European Elder (Sambucus nigra) and Common Elder (S. canadensis). Both of these elders are hardy shrubs with strongly scented flowers arranged in bunches. The leaves are dark green, and the black berries produced in late summer are greatly enjoyed by many kinds of birds as well as humans! An important point about elders is that they are particularly attractive to aphids, which feed and multiply on the young, growing shoots. Small birds, especially finches, thoroughly check all the branches looking for aphids and small spiders. If you keep small tropical birds with your cockatiels, it is almost essential to provide them regularly with aphid-infested elder branches, especially during the breeding season.

European Hornbeam *(Carpinus betulus)*. This species makes an ideal hedge in which the birds—I am again thinking of small exotic birds—like to build their nests. The oval leaves are clearly doubly indented and attached to short little stems. The leaves turn a beautiful brownish yellow in the winter. Since they do not drop off for a long time, they lend some protection from the wind and rain. Once temperatures drop below freezing, however, the leaves will fall quite quickly. As a tree, this species can grow to a height of 35–45 feet (10–14 m).

European Larch *(Larix decidua)*. The soft, light-green needles, over 1 inch (3 cm) in length, are shed in the fall and are placed in small groups in cuplike sheaths. This species will do well even in the poor soil often found inside an aviary.

Nordmann's Fir *(Abies nordmanniana)*. The needles of this fir are striking and shiny. About 1 inch (2–3 cm) long, they are attached in a brushlike arrangement. The egg-shaped buds do not secrete resin. In its young form, this evergreen makes an ideal aviary plant. Although it originated in Asia Minor and the Causasus, Nordmann's fir is grown extensively in many parts of the world.

Oregon Holly-Grape *(Mahonia aquifolium)*. This is a commonly cultivated North American shrub. Growing to a height of just over 3 feet (1 m), it is of ideal size for the aviary. Its bullet-shaped, dark-blue berries are enjoyed by the birds, which helps make it a good choice. The oval leaves, which have rather prickly teeth, are a beautiful red in summer, turning blackish red in the winter. The Oregon holly-grape will do well in almost any location and any soil.

Oriental Arborvitae *(Thuja orientalis)*. The leaves are green on both sides and are arranged in similar symmetry to those of the preceding species. Originating in China and Japan, it is now grown in great numbers elsewhere. Wild specimens can also be found in Iran.

Scotch Pine *(Pinus silvestris)*. This tree is very common in sandy soil areas and on moors. It will also do well in the aviary, particularly small specimens under 3 feet (90 cm) high. It is an evergreen. The firm needles grow in small bunches (two needles), are bluish green in color, and can grow to 3 inches (8 cm) in length. The bud is reddish brown and seldom secretes resin.

Silver Fir *(Abies alba, also Picea abies)*. The needles of the silver fir are a shiny, dark green on the top side, with two bluish white stripes running along the bottom side. The buds are light brown and do not feel sticky, since they do not secrete any resin. The needles are about 1 inch (2–3 cm) long and are individually attached. This evergreen tree is particularly attractive and decorative when still young and will do well even in poor sandy soils.

Spruce *(Picea excelsa)*. The needles, a little less than 1 inch (2 cm) in length, are individually attached to each branch. Dark green in color, the

Common Poisonous Outdoor Plants

American Yew	*(Taxus canadensis)*	Indian Turnip	*(Arisaema triphyllum)*
Baneberry	*(Actaea* species)	Iris	*(Iris* species)
Bittersweet		Jack-in-the-Pulpit	*(Arisaema triphyllum)*
Nightshade	*(Solanum dulcamara)*	Jimsonweed	*(Datura* species)
Black Locust	*(Robinia pseudoacacia)*	Larkspur	*(Delphinium* species)
Bloodroot	*(Sanguinario* species)	Locoweed	*(Astragalus mollissimus)*
Buckthorn	*(Rhamnus* species)	Lords and Ladies	*(Arum* species)
Buttercup	*(Ranunculus* species)	May Apple	*(Podophyllum* species)
Calla Lily	*(Zantedeschia*	Mistletoe	
	aethiopica)	(only the berries)	*(Santalales* species)
Cherry Tree	*(Prunus* species)	Monkshood	*(Aconitum* species)
Christmas Candle	*(Pedilanthus*	Morning Glory	*(Ipomoea* species)
	tithymaloides)	Mountain Laurel	*(Kalmia latifolia)*
Clematis	*(Clematis* species)	Nutmeg	*(Myristica fragrans)*
Cowslip	*(Caltha* species)	Pokeweed	*(Phytolacca amaricana)*
Daphne	*(Daphne* species)	Rhubarb	*(Rheum rhaponticum)*
English Yew	*(Taxus baccata)*	Rosary Peas	*(Abrus precatorius)*
Golden Chain		Snowdrop	*(Galanthus nivalis)*
or Laburnum	*(Laburnum anagyroides)*	Snowflake	*(Leucoium vernum)*
Hemlock	*(Conium maculatum)*	Sweet Pea	*(Lathyrus latifolius)*
Henbane	*(Hyoscyamus niger)*	Tobacco	*(Nicotiana* species)
Honey Locust	*(Gleditsia triacathos)*	Water Hemlock	*(Cicuta maculata)*
Horse Chestnut	*(Aesculus* species)	Western Yew	*(Taxus breviflora)*

buds have no resin. Branches grow right to the base of the straight trunk, particularly in specimens subject to direct light. Also contributing to this tree's popularity is the fact that it is a very hardy evergreen.

Apart from all of the above, there are many other choices (actually the choices are endless, especially if we were to take climatic zones into consideration), such as: all *Cornus* (dogwood) species, the mock orange

Common potentially poisonous houseplants. Top right: rhododendron; bottom left: caladium; bottom right: dieffenbachia.

(Philadelphus coronarius), the Viburnum species, and sea buckthorn (Hippophae rhamnoides). Also good are various Vaccinum species, such as the highbush blueberry, whartleberry, or swamp blueberry (V. corymbosum), the cranberry (V. macrocarpon), the lowbush blueberry (V. pennsylvanicum or V. augustifolium), and the cowberry or foxberry (V. vitisidaea). Then there are various Genistra species, including the African broom (G. monosperma), creeping broom (G. sagittalis), and dyer's greenweed (G. tinctoria). Also, do not forget the Cotoneaster species.

Grass sods placed on the aviary floor are very good. If the grass is watered regularly, you are very likely to see your cockatiels frolicking in it . . . a very pleasant sight indeed. Tropical finches also enjoy grass sods and will seek out insects and the like in it. Many birds lie in the grass to sunbathe.

Keeping the Cage Clean

Good hygiene will go a long way toward keeping your birds in prime health. A bird kept in a dirty, dusty cage will soon become ill. The cage, perches, water and food containers, bath, holders for cuttlebone and greens, and other appurtenances must all be kept scrupulously clean. It is best to make this cleaning a routine habit—for example, once a week on Saturday afternoon. Once a month everything should be thoroughly disinfected. For this chore you would normally have to remove the birds from the cage (but not if the birds are breeding!). If a second cage is available, letting the washed cage and its perches dry in direct sunlight is an excellent natural method of killing germs. The cage should be cleaned using warm, soapy water, then rinsed with cold water, so that disease-carrying organisms are not given a chance to set up home. The same procedure applies to various pieces of equipment that belong in the cage. Glass, plastic, or porcelain feeders that are cracked or have pieces chipped off should be replaced. It is in such locations that potentially dangerous organisms often gather and sooner or later launch their attack!

The Sand Tray

As mentioned earlier, every well-constructed cage should have its floor covered by a sand tray that can be pulled out, so that the floor can be cleaned frequently with minimum disturbance to the birds. Cages available in pet shops and that are made primarily of wire bars usually have a removable base. It is best to first cover the cage bottom or tray with a piece of strong paper (brown wrapping paper is ideal) cut to the exact size. Special, sterilized bird sand (shell sand or grit) that can be obtained from your pet store should be placed in a layer ¾ to 1½ inches (2–3 cm) deep on top of the paper. The paper and the sand should be

45

removed and replaced at least once a week. In order to minimize kicking sand out of the cage, it is advisable to affix a piece of glass or plastic about 4 inches (10 cm) high around the bottom of the cage. Many decorative cages are available with this convenience already added, but often the tower-type cages are not so equipped. As mentioned, I do not recommend this design, but those who use cages of this type will have to improvise something in place of these glass or plastic shields.

Basic Grooming

Baths

Wild cockatiels like to "roll" around in moist grass. In the early morning, when the grass is still covered with dew, this little scene can give bird watchers a great deal of pleasure. However, such a sight is very rare among captive birds. Still, all cockatiels enjoy a water bath, which should be offered in a shallow ceramic or metal dish. There will be very few days that your cockatiel does not make grateful use of the bath. The birds can also be sprayed using a mister filled with tepid water.

If you are exhibiting your birds, they will need to be given a bath about a week or so before the show. Before removing the bird from its cage, fill two shallow bowls with warm water (about 57°F [25°C]), dissolving a little mild soap in one of the bowls. Now hold the bird in your hand so that your thumb and forefinger can support its little head and keep it in the right direction. Carefully lower the bird into the soapy water, ensuring that its head does not get wet and that soap does not get into its eyes, nose, or beak. After dunking your bird a few times in this fashion, wet an old, soft-haired shaving brush (or something similar, as shaving brushes are sometimes hard to find) in soapy water and brush the plumage in the direction of the tail. Be sure not to forget the area around the vent. Clean the head and neck with a soft sponge. Do a good job on the wing feathers, spreading them on the edge of the bowl and stroking them with the brush. Clean the tail in the same manner, but always be gentle in order to avoid the accidental

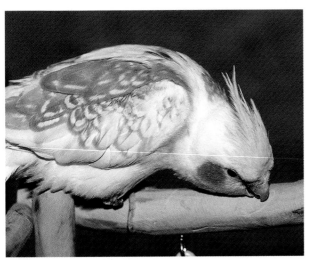

A beautiful fawn pied cockatiel. The fawn mutation in Europe is known as cinnamon and isabelle, but because we are dealing with so-called ground birds (as opposed to yellow ground birds) they should really be termed "fawn" like we do in, for example, zebra finches and canaries, where a white ground is also involved.

removal of feathers. Then dunk the bird a few times in the bowl of clean water to remove all traces of the soap, and brush the plumage back into shape with a thoroughly rinsed brush. (You can imagine that all this handling will put your bird's feathers a little out of kilter!)

Conclude the operation by drying your bird with a thick towel that has been heated just a little (perhaps in a clothes dryer or by hanging it over the radiator for a few minutes). Do not rub the feathers; just wrap the bird in the towel and dab gently. When the bird is touch-dry, place it in a clean cage (without sand) in an adequately heated room (never outside in the sun!). Here the bird should stay until the next day to ensure that it will not catch cold. The room should not be too warm, however, because that may cause the feathers to curl, which, of course, is not the idea. The bird itself will help the drying process by fluffing, shaking, and preening its feathers. A hair dryer may be of service if you wish the bird to dry quickly, but the setting should be on low and it should be used with care.

Nail and Beak Trimming

Nails and beaks are generally kept in good natural trim if cockatiels have regular access to wooden perches of various thicknesses, fresh tree branches, cuttlefish bone, and similar items. In the outside or garden aviary, provide some rough stones that birds can use as natural nail trimmers.

A daily spray will help to keep the cockatiel's plumage in excellent condition. Afterward, the bird will help the drying process by preening its feathers.

If, despite these precautions, you notice a bird developing overly long nails, you must trim them. Catch and hold the bird—but not on its back to avoid stress and shock. Hold the bird up against the light so that you can see the blood vessels outlined against the horn of the nails. You don't want to cut this pink area (called the *quick*).

While holding the bird in the palm of your hand, grasp the bird's leg between your index and middle finger. If possible, have an assistant use an extremely sharp pair of nail clippers, and cut just short of the quick. (If the nails are dark colored, clip only very small pieces during one "operation.") Sometimes a capillary grows along with the nail. Have a styptic pencil or cotton on hand to deal with this minor mishap.

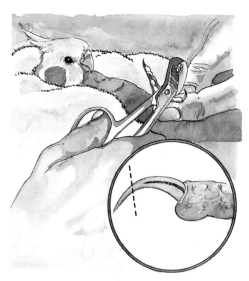

Nail clipping. Be careful not to cut the part that is supplied with blood (the "quick"), but if the nail does start to bleed, a moistened styptic pencil should be applied to the bleeding end. Note the proper restraining method. If you are inexperienced, work with a helper and wear leather gloves. Better still, assign the job to your veterinarian.

Beak trimming should be left in the hands of an experienced aviculturist or avian veterinarian.

Special Care Considerations

Free Flight Indoors

Most cockatiel owners like to allow their birds to fly freely in one of the rooms of the house for a few hours each day. However, there are certain precautions you should take before letting the bird out of its cage. Ensure that all windows are closed and covered with drapes. Since birds cannot see the glass in the windows, closed drapes can prevent the serious, even fatal, accidents that occur when a bird crashes against window glass. Electrical appliances such as electric ranges and especially fans should be turned off when your bird is out of its cage. A ceiling fan represents a particularly lethal source of danger to a free-flying bird. Make sure your fireplace is well protected with a fine-mesh guard. Remember that cockatiels have been known to disappear up the chimney even when there is no fire!

Indoor plants and cut flowers can cause problems to birds and, of course, to the plants themselves. Cockatiels find it hard to resist nibbling at house plants, some of which are poisonous; others, such as cacti, can cause nasty wounds. It is therefore advisable to remove all plants from the room or to cover them with plastic.

During the Summer Months

The cockatiel keeper—or the keeper of any bird or animal species, for that matter—should remember that it is very important to keep food dishes and sleeping quarters as clean as possible. During the warmer months of the year, some of the soft foods (universal food, egg food, rearing food, bread that has been soaked in water or milk, green foods, etc.) spoil very fast. On hot days it is best to prepare no more soft food than can be consumed in an hour or so. Any residue should then be discarded and fresh food prepared for the next meal. High temperatures allow many damaging insects to breed rapidly, and encourage the growth of bacteria.

It is also important for birds that spend the better part of the year indoors to be taken outside once in a while, cage and all, during the spring and summer. Do not place the cage in the direct rays of the sun, of course. Even birds that live out of doors may be subject to sunstroke! Keep your birds more or less in the shade, in an area safe from cats, dogs, and other bird enemies. If you keep cats, constant alertness will very likely be necessary. If you spend some time outside with your birds, they will very much enjoy romping on the grass if you place the cage, with its tray removed, on the lawn.

During the Evening and at Night

Cockatiels need to have 10 to 12 hours of rest each day. Therefore, do not expose your bird to too much noise. If you have a television in the same room as the cage, the best thing to do is shield the cage with a cloth at the appropriate times. A cage with one or more cockatiels should in any case never be placed near to a television set. Although it may be impossible for people to detect the rapid changes of dot patterns on the color TV screen, most birds see this and it is bad for their eyes. The farther away the cage is placed from the TV, the less damage will be inflicted.

A cockatiel that is housed inside, just like this white face cinnamon pearl one, should have at least 10–12 hours of rest each day. It is therefore often necessary to cover the cage with some kind of cloth (covers are available commercially) during the latter part of the evening and at night, especially when the cage is located in a living room or den where a lot of activity is going on.

Many bird fanciers maintain that a cage should be completely covered with some kind of cloth during the evening and at night. However, not every cockatiel is thrilled with this arrangement. I believe that the best method is to cover just one side and/or the top of the cage so that no direct light or TV emissions shine onto the cage bird. Thus, the bird may decide for itself whether to sit in the light or not!

Table of Dangers

Source of Danger	Effects (Remedy)
Bathroom	Open windows: bird escapes; cleansers and chemicals: poisoning; open toilet bowl: drowning. (Keep bathroom door closed.)
Cage and aviary mesh with wrong sized openings	Cockatiel sticks head through mesh or between bars, gets caught, suffers injury, or strangles to death. (Check mesh size with pet dealer.)
Water containers (sinks, tubs, aquariums, vases, toilet bowl)	Cockatiel falls in and drowns. Bird can mistake foam on the surface as a firm landing place. (Keep containers empty and/or covered.)
Direct sunlight	Heatstroke: Heavy panting, extended wings, weakness, collapse. (Get bird into shade immediately to prevent heart failure. Give patient some water and see an avian veterinarian immediately.)
Doors	Cockatiel gets caught in them and is crushed or escapes. (Close door before releasing bird.)
Drafts (open doors and windows, airing the room, etc.)	Colds; nasal discharges, runny eyes, sneezing, pneumonia. (Avoid drafts; remove bird when room is being aired.)
Drawers, cupboards	Cockatiels are curious and like to explore open drawers and cabinets. If a bird is accidentally shut inside, it can starve to death or suffocate. (Keep drawers and cupboards closed.)
Easy chairs, couches, etc.	Cockatiels can be crushed when accidentally sat on. (Get in the habit of checking chairs before sitting down.)
Electrical wires and sockets	Shock from biting through wires; death. (Conceal wires under moldings, carpets, etc.)
Hard floors	Cockatiels with clipped wings lack full powers of flight. Such birds can break a leg or bruise themselves in a hard landing. (See discussion of clipped wings, page 86.)
Human feet	Free cockatiel can get stepped on. (Look before you walk.)
Kitchen	Never keep your cockatiel in an area that is polluted by gas and cooking fumes. Fumes given off by overheated or burning Teflon® pans are toxic to birds. Also dangerous are steam and heat from cooking; open pots containing hot liquids; hot stoves; and household cleansers, all of which are potentially poisonous. (Keep birds out of kitchen.)

Table of Dangers (continued)

Source of Danger	Effects (Remedy)
Knitted or crocheted items, yarn, string, chains	The cockatiel's toes can get entangled; trapped bird can strangle itself. (Remove sweaters, yarn, etc.)
Large decorative vases	Cockatiels can slip in and not be able to climb out again; suffocation, starvation, heart failure. (Fill these containers with sand or paper.)
Nicotine, sprays, etc.	Smoke-laden air is harmful; nicotine is lethal. Other dangerous air pollutants for birds are: paint fumes, carbon monoxide, insecticide sprays, deodorizer sprays, and insecticidal pest strips. (Do not smoke, use sprays, etc. near your birds.)
Perches too small in diameter	Excessive growth of toenails. (Use hardwood perches of correct diameter. See page 21.)
Pesticides	All pesticides are lethal for birds. (Never spray plants in the room where your bird is kept or bring sprayed plants into that room.)
Poisons	Deadly: lead, rust, pans coated with plastics, mercury, all household cleansers. Harmful: pencil leads, inserts for ballpoint pens, magic markers, alcohol, coffee, hot spices. Other poisons: acetone, amphetamines, aspirin, antifreeze, arsenic, bleach, carbon tetrachloride, chlordane, cosmetics, crayons, DDT, deodorants, drain cleaners, fabric softeners, firecrackers, fluoroacetates, garbage toxins, hair dye, linoleum, lye, matches (the so-called safety matches are nontoxic), medicines, mothballs, various wild mushrooms, lead-based paint, perfume, petroleum products, pine oil, rat and mouse poison, red squill, roach poison, shellac, sleeping pills, snail bait, strychnine, suntan lotions, thallium, Warfarin® and weed killers, wood preservatives. (Remove all harmful and lethal substances.)
Sharp objects, nails, splinters, ends of wire	Cuts, puncture wounds. (Remove all sharp objects.)
Temperature changes	Cockatiel will do well in 50 to 75°F (10–24°C). Abrupt changes in temperature can be disastrous for your birds. (The heating should be even and reliable.)
Windows, picture windows, glass walls	Cockatiel flies into them: concussion, fractured skull, broken neck, wings, or feet. (Lower shades, cover with draperies.)

Chapter Three
Foods and Feeding

There are six fundamental elements essential to the diet of all animals, including human beings: proteins, carbohydrates, fats, vitamins, minerals, and water. Let us briefly examine each of these dietary constituents and discuss their merits.

Proteins

The bodies of all animals are composed mainly of various forms of protein; each body is made up of millions and millions of cells, each containing protoplasm, which itself is composed chiefly of proteins and water. A bird's muscles, internal organs (such as heart and kidneys), feathers, skin, feet, beak, and of course eggs, all are rich in protein. In brief, proteins are essential for the growth, maintenance, and repair of all body tissues, for proper organic functions, and for reproduction.

There are two main categories of proteins: animal and vegetable. Animal proteins have a greater nutritional value than plant proteins. The most important sources of animal protein are meat, fish, eggs, and milk. For instance, poultry breeders feed a supplement of fish-meal and liver-meal as a source of animal protein for their birds. Milk is the simplest and most-often used source of protein.

Stale wheat bread soaked in milk is an excellent food for cockatiels throughout the year, but especially in the breeding season. Once accustomed to it, the birds not only will eat it readily but will also feed it enthusiastically to their offspring. Such a meal should be given only in the mornings. What has not been consumed by midday should be removed and disposed of, since such a mixture will sour very quickly. Nevertheless, many birds are sensitive to milk sugar, which is present in milk (not, however, in cultured milk products such as yogurt!) and which they are not able to break down. This could give rise to digestive upsets.

In addition to bread and milk, protein can be fed to birds in the form of freshly caught insects or commercially available, high-protein concentrated (universal) food or rearing food.

Cockatiels obtain most of their vegetable protein from the great variety of seeds and green food that should be offered to them. Of all green foods, birds seem to like lettuce the best. (Lettuce and similar greens should be washed and dried thoroughly before being fed to your birds, to remove any impurities.) Other green foods that find favor among cockatiels are endive, curly kale, parsley, sprouting seeds, brussels sprouts, spinach, celery, chicory, cabbage heart, cucumber, Swiss chard, watercress, turnip greens, and zucchini.

Green food is composed principally of water. (I once conducted an experiment with parakeets—a species that is known to subsist well in drought conditions—in which they were given only a few drops of drinking water over a period of months. Being fed on adequate green food, the birds remained in good health; they obtained almost all their water supply from the greens and, to a lesser extent, from some other foods in their diet.) Since water content is so high, there is not much room left in greens for proteins. In fact, the protein content of green food is usually between 1.5 percent and 4.5 percent. Young, green shoots are normally richer in protein than full-grown leaves. Young leaves of spinach, lettuce, and sprouting seeds are much more nutritious than older leaves.

During the summer, green food will gradually lose its nutritive value unless you plant small quantities of

Remember that a high quality diet is vitally important to the degree of success of the bird lover's efforts. So this means that the food composition for cockatiels must contain every conceivable nutrient necessary for their growth and energy supply.

seed at regular intervals so that you have a regular supply of young growth. However, an important point to remember is that ripe seed has a greater percentage of protein than unripe seed.

Feathers, beak, and nails are composed mainly of keratin, which is in turn largely protein. It is therefore obvious that nestlings and fledglings, as they grow and form plumage, must have a good supply of protein-rich food. A deficiency in the protein supply will have a much more drastic effect on growing birds than on adults. A shortage of protein in young birds will also diminish the nutritive value of any other dietary elements they may be receiving. Many difficulties in birds, such as feather plucking and even cannibalism, can be related to a deficiency of protein in the diet. (Of course, protein deficiency is not always the cause of these problems, but it is one of the factors an experienced bird owner will take into account.)

It is important that a variety of protein sources be used, as each source can have a different composition. Even foodstuffs that are apparently the same can vary in composition, depending on the area from which they came and the manner in which they were produced. This fact is especially evident in vegetable protein. For example, it is estimated that the protein content of a good, standard cockatiel seed mixture could vary between 16 percent and 19 percent. It must be realized, however, that such protein can be utilized in the body to best advantage if it is accompanied by an adequate intake of vitamins and minerals.

One more point: All insects have a hard, chitinous outer layer that is barely digestible, though it is composed largely of protein. Try to feed your birds insects (or other invertebrates) with a softer skin. Mealworms, enchytrae (whiteworms),

flies, their larvae, and similar bugs are therefore preferable to beetles and ants.

Carbohydrates

Carbohydrates are a combination of the elements carbon, hydrogen, and oxygen. They are produced by plants in the presence of sunlight during the process called photosynthesis. All carbohydrates start as simple sugars, or monosaccharides ($C_6H_{12}O_6$). With combination, the more complex di-, tri-, and polysaccharides are produced. Glucose and fructose are common monosaccharides; refined cane sugar, or sucrose ($C_{12}H_{22}O_{11}$) is a disaccharide; starch is a polysaccharide. Too much carbohydrate, from grains such as corn and whole oats, can be bad for your cockatiel's plumage.

Fats and Oils

There are two primary sources of fat in a bird's diet. In addition to the fat quantities contained in seed, the carbohydrates in foods such as corn can also be converted into fat in the body. In general, these two sources are adequate for the needs of cage and aviary birds, especially if you regularly add a few drops of fish-liver oil to the birds' seed (approximately 4 drops to 2 pounds [907 g]). Too much fat can be as harmful to birds as too little. Birds that become too fat seldom make good breeders and are likely to have bad molts. This can be a problem, especially in cage birds, which may get minimum exercise, or in birds that are overfed carbohydrate-containing seeds such as hemp.

Another danger is that a diet high in fat will result in the bird's stomach becoming "lazy," so that all digestion takes place in the intestines. Different bird species have varied requirements regarding quantities of fat in the diet. In addition, the climate in which the bird lives will dictate the type and quantity of seeds it must eat. During the cold winter months, a greater amount of fat is required than during the summer.

Fortunately, most kinds of bird seed in general use do not have a high fat content. Canary grass seed has 4 to 6 percent, millet, milo, and oats about 4 percent. As mentioned above, hemp has a high fat content—about 26 percent, the same as sunflower seed. These percentages can vary, but they are a good average. The method of harvesting, thrashing, etc., can affect the nutritional content. Green food is low in fat, with an average of just 0.3 percent.

Vitamins

Vitamins are probably the most important micronutrients for humans and animals. Without vitamins, life itself is impossible. Yet vitamins have been intensively studied only since 1912.

Vitamins are broadly divided into two groups, the fat-soluble and the water-soluble vitamins. As vitamins A, D, E, and K are found in various oils and fats, they belong to the former category, while vitamins C and the various B-complex vitamins, being found in water-containing substances, belong to the latter category. Only a tiny quantity of each of the essential vitamins is necessary to keep the body in good health. However, a deficiency of one or more will lead to various physical problems and diseases.

Fat-soluble Vitamins

Vitamin A: Vitamin A is fundamental to the correct function of body cell metabolism, the maintenance of skin and mucous membranes, and the enhancement of sight. Vitamin A also has influence on the respiratory system and plays a part in the pigmentation of the retina, thus allowing the eye to function well in poor light.

By far the best source of vitamin A is cod-liver oil. Foods that contain vitamin A and that you can give to your birds include milk, egg yolk, fresh greens (especially spinach), parsley, lettuce, and dandelion (finely chopped). Greens and various roots (carrots) contain carotene, from which birds can then manufacture vitamin A. In general, seeds are low in vitamin A content, and birds that are fed on only a seed diet will sooner or later suffer from a vitamin A deficiency.

Yellow corn, rape seed, and yellow millet are some of the seeds that hold significant and usable quantities of vitamin A. The yellow color indicates the presence of provitamin A (carotene), which is also common in carrots.

Birds in breeding season require a vitamin A supply many times greater than their nonbreeding neighbors. Although the birds do not inevitably become sterile because of vitamin A deficiency, they will produce weak youngsters, and brooding problems will be the order of the day.

Vitamin A is not only called the anti-infection or growth vitamin, it is also called the anti-sterility or fertility vitamin, a name also given mistakenly to vitamin D (see next section). Various preparations of vitamin A/D are available on the market under various trade names. Although excess A and D are disposed of in the bird's liver, one should be aware that an overdose can result in fading of the plumage (vitamin A) or decalcification of the bones (vitamin D).

A combination vitamin A/D preparation should be administered daily by mixing it in with the seed and thus diluting its strength. Healthy birds should be given a preventive dose of 4 drops of fish-liver oil in 2 pounds (907 g) of seed. If a bird has never received supplementary doses of vitamins A/D, it is advisable to start the treatment with 5 or 6 drops mixed well with the seed. A bird with a mild deficiency, or one that has been deficient for only a short time, should show signs of returning to full health after a week; serious cases

may take a month or longer or, alas, may never be cured. Crusty discharges around the beak may be washed away with lukewarm water.

Birds with a deficiency of vitamin A are usually also deficient in other vitamins. In such cases, a small amount of powdered yeast (on the tip of a knife) can be added to 2 pounds (907 g) of seed mixture treated with fish-liver oil. Keep an eye on the droppings. If they do become abnormal, the treatment should be stopped.

Vitamin D: This vitamin is also known as the sunshine vitamin or sometimes as the antirickets vitamin. Fish-liver oils probably have the highest vitamin D content, followed by egg yolk and milk. The best source of vitamin D by far is sunshine, which activates the provitamins in the birds' skin.

If birds are kept in well-designed outside aviaries during the summer (or perhaps all year round in mild climates), it is not generally necessary for them to receive supplementary vitamin D. Birds that are kept indoors should receive supplements of fish-liver oil or the commercial vitamin A/D drops that come under various brand names.

Birds that have never had cod-liver oil should be introduced to it gradually (first, 3 drops to 2 pounds [907 g] of seed, then gradually increase). Birds that are kept in outside aviaries and have access to unfiltered sunlight do not need a vitamin D supplement except during the breeding season.

At one time, it was thought that seed treated with cod-liver oil would quickly become rancid. This is not the case! It takes a long time for cod-liver oil to turn rancid at room temperature. In laboratory tests, it took 300 hours for cod-liver oil to turn rancid under a temperature of 194°F.

There are many other vitamin preparations that you can use as a substitute for cod-liver oil. Over the years I have experimented with many of these preparations, and I can assure you that they are all reliable, provided you follow the manufacturer's instructions that are printed on the package.

Vitamin E: This vitamin, like vitamin A, is often called the anti-sterility or fertility vitamin, although its function is not so much concerned with fertility as with the normal growth and development of the embryo and hatchling. Natural vitamin E is found in adequate quantities in germinated bird seed. Wheat germ oil and corn germ oil are excellent sources of vitamin E. The edible green leaves of many plants (lettuce, watercress, spinach, kale, etc.) are also a good source; Vitamin E also occurs in the yolk of eggs but is absent from cod-liver oil.

Vitamin E is necessary for the development of the skeletal muscles, the nerve cells of the brain, the protein content of the blood, the correct function of the sperm-producing parts of the testes, and especially for the overall development and growth of the embryo. This vitamin should never be absent from a bird's diet. In feeding your birds, never give rancid food, always use the recommended wheat germ oil or germinated rape seed, and be careful not to give an overdose of, for example, hemp; moderation is the rule! Too much hemp can cause avitaminosis E, which can seriously affect a bird's fertility and disturb the nervous system.

Vitamin K: This vitamin is known primarily as the blood-clotting vitamin (K is from the Danish *Koagulation*). Normally, bird fanciers do not have problems with deficiencies of this vitamin if their birds receive a balanced diet. Green food, carrot tops, kale, alfalfa, liver, soy beans, and some grains have a high vitamin K content. Vitamin K, unlike most other vitamins, is not destroyed by heating. Most seeds (with the exception of hemp) are poorly supplied with vitamin K.

The most obvious sign of a vitamin K deficiency is internal or external bleeding. Various bird species have different reactions to a vitamin K deficiency. Turkeys and other gallinaceous birds sometimes have trouble with bleeding feet, wings, and tails; cockatiels and other parrot-like birds bleed under the skin, especially on the rump and tail.

Water-soluble Vitamins

At the present time, some 14 components of the vitamin B-complex are recognized, and it is likely that more will be discovered in the future. These vitamins are very important for cockatiels and other pet birds and, fortunately, are contained in the seeds that are a normal part of a bird's diet.

Thiamine (Vitamin B1): Excellent sources of thiamine are the germ cells of grain seeds, legume seeds, and brewer's yeast (and other yeast preparations); smaller amounts of thiamine are found in meat, powdered milk, and eggs. The seed husk also contains thiamine, but this is not efficiently used by birds unless they have the advantage of getting very young, unripe seed as part of their diet. Fruit and green food also contain small amounts of thiamine.

Riboflavin (B2 or G): This vitamin is associated with growth and is contained mainly in yeast. Green leaves, powdered milk, and eggs are also good sources. Good quality seeds have an adequate quantity of this vitamin in the germ. Other good sources are yeast, liver, egg yolk, and seeds (especially sunflower and peanuts). A varied ration of green food each day will prevent any mishaps. An inadequate intake of riboflavin in the diet will lead to inefficient egg production, deaths in the shell, inflammation of the feet, twisted toes, poor down and feather development, inflamed skin, scabs around the nostrils, and other problems.

Choline: A deficiency of this vitamin coupled with a shortage of manganese leads to a fatty liver. In the poultry industry this problem is commonly referred to as perosis. Choline is found largely in the linings of the intestines, where it plays an important part in the maintenance of peristaltic contractions. It also regulates the transport of fatty acids and the breaking down of them in the liver.

A deficiency of this vitamin is not so common among cockatiels as among other cage and aviary birds, but a few cases occur from time to time. In general, a deficiency causes inflammation and swelling of all the joints in nestling birds. The birds cannot hold themselves in a normal position, resulting in malformed growth. A deficiency can also cause internal disturbances that lead to the laying of poor and few eggs. To avoid this and other vitamin deficiencies, give the birds seed of the highest quality and a variety of green food, and do not give soft food that contains few vitamins. Rich sources of choline are liver, brewer's yeast, fishmeal, and grains.

Biotin: This vitamin is sometimes referred to as vitamin H and is, in my opinion, one of the most important vitamins for cockatiels and other psittacines. A deficiency causes symptoms that are remarkably similar to French molt, which is common in parakeets.

Biotin is very soluble in water, making it very easy to administer. (Never mix it with raw egg white.) The greatest percentage of biotin is contained in egg yolk, but liver, pancreas, kidneys, cow's milk, yeast, tomatoes, peanuts, pulses, carrots, and spinach are also important sources. Fresh seeds contain adequate amounts of biotin, but of course the quantity varies from type to type.

Vitamin B12 (Cyanocobalamine or Cobalamine): This vitamin contains traces of cobalt and phosphorus and stimulates growth, particularly of feathers, and plays an important role in the synthesis of protein, the creation of blood, and the formulation of methionine from cystine. The best sources are liver, fishmeal, other animal products, yeast, and milk products. B12 can also be synthetically manufactured and stored in crystalline form. It should never be added to the food, however, as the quantity must be scientifically regulated to prevent an overdose.

Vitamin C: Natural vitamin C is also known as ascorbic acid. It is essential for humans as well as cockatiels, but unlike us, the birds are able to manufacture the vitamin synthetically during their process of digestion. It is therefore not necessary to give cockatiels a vitamin C supplement except in more or less unusual situations, such as when a bird is afflicted by diseases or poisoning, when birds are in traveling cages or in exhibitions, and in other special circumstances.

Vitamin C cannot be stored in the body, so any excess is soon lost. It is known that young cockatiels and parakeets are born with adequate vitamin C and, according to G.S. Binks, do not require any for the first two to three months of life. After this period, however, they must receive adequate vitamin C, or else their feet will swell, their breathing become difficult, and, if held in the hand, they will give the impression of being in permanent pain. (One may also note that the pupils are enlarged.) In general, such birds will be very weak, but when they are given access to vitamin C, their condition will improve in a few days. Commercial food containing vitamin C, but especially fruits with a high vitamin C content—oranges and other citrus fruits, for example—are absolutely essential in such cases.

Minerals

It is well known that minerals should be present in a bird's diet. The most important mineral is calcium (Ca); without it, for example, it would be impossible for the hen to form eggs. Some of the other minerals that can be found in a bird's diet are phosphorus (P), sodium (Na), chlorine (Cl), potassium (K), magnesium (Mg), iron (Fe), zinc (Zn), copper (Cu), sulphur (S), iodine (I), and manganese (Mn).

Calcium and Phosphorus

Calcium is very important in the manufacture and maintenance of the skeleton, in blood coagulation, in the functioning of sinews and organs such as the heart, and in the formation of the eggshell. Phosphorus also plays an important role in the formation and the maintenance of the skeletal structure, and in bodily metabolism; it may also be an ingredient of protein or fat. A bird's body requires about three times as much calcium as phosphorus. It is important that a balance exist between these two minerals, or the bodily functions will be disturbed, frequently with disastrous consequences. You need not worry too much about phosphorus, since it is contained in adequate amounts of green food and seeds, especially in bran. (Seed husks are also a good source, but they are not eaten by cockatiels.) Adequate calcium supplements should be available to your cockatiels at all times. Good sources include dicalcium phosphate, chalk, cuttlebone, grit (including finely ground shells), ground eggshells (sterilized), and powdered limestone. Calcium salt is called calcium carbonate; it is quickly absorbed during digestion and efficiently used by the birds. Oyster grit, according to C. Feyerabend, has probably the highest percentage of calcium, with about 86 percent calcium carbonate. Cuttlebone contains about 81.5 percent calcium carbonate, and the birds will take it readily. An advantage of cuttlebone is that it can be stored for years without losing any of its qualities, as long as it is kept in a clean, dry place. When you put it in the cage or aviary, hang it where there is little danger that it can be contaminated with droppings. Contaminated cuttlebone is hazardous. If it does become soiled, scrub it in clean water. Moreover, it should be placed in the covered part of the aviary, where it can remain dry; rain will spoil it.

An old piece of builders' lime will also be utilized by most cockatiels.

It has the additional advantage of keeping the birds' beaks in trim (the same can be said of cuttlebone). A shortage of calcium in a bird's diet can lead to coprophagy, the practice of eating one's own droppings. If a bird's diet is in good order, then this problem should never arise— but if it does, reassess the seed mixtures and ensure that the birds have permanent access to cuttlebone, grit, calcium blocks, or other sources of the mineral. At one time it was thought that birds required mineral supplements only during the molt, but scientific research has proven that birds require minerals the whole year round. If a bird refuses to use the cuttlebone or other calcium supplement, crush it to a powder that can be mixed in with the seed menu and/or sprinkle on the floor of the cage or aviary. Do this only if the birds really do not gnaw at the bone or block, as we know that this helps to keep the beaks in good shape.

It is necessary to give the birds a good choice of mineral sources well before the start of the breeding season, so that the hens are able to form the eggs. During the rearing of the chicks, calcium-containing material is important for the development of the skeleton and other parts of the body.

Other Minerals

Research has shown that a little magnesium in the birds' diet helps to maintain the correct balance of calcium, phosphorus, and vitamin D.

A deficiency of magnesium leads to convulsions, stunted growth, and sparse feathering. Magnesium is found in seeds, especially wheat, and in many nuts.

Cockatiels also require iodine, copper, and many other minerals, mostly in very small quantities. Most of these essential minerals are contained in the normal foodstuffs, including seeds and green food. Small amounts of iodine are contained in cuttlebone, seashell grit, oyster shells, meat, milk, and eggs. Fishmeal and cod-liver oil are rich in iodine; wheat germ oil is not. With our recommended regular feeding of stale wheat bread soaked in milk, your birds should not be troubled with an iodine deficiency (which causes goiter).

Potassium, sodium, and iron will restrict some parasites. Sodium helps coordinate tissue construction and neutralizes the carbon dioxide that is produced, and helps ensure the assimilation of food. Magnesium (along with calcium) is necessary for the formation of bone.

Iron and manganese in the red blood cells bind the oxygen from the air taken into the lungs and promote a good circulation. Sulphur and silicon help in the formation of the plumage.

Copper is necessary for the efficient manufacture of blood. It also activates the absorption of iron (via the intestines) and plays a part in the manufacture of hemoglobin in blood. A shortage of copper results in anemia.

Insoluble Grit

A good grit mixture is absolutely essential for cockatiels. Insoluble grit assists the gizzard muscles in the grinding of food, such as seed. There are various grit mixtures available. Sea sand and ground granite are insoluble in the stomach and act as grindstones until they are worn small enough to be passed through the system. (Soluble grit, including oyster shells, cuttlebone, and sterilized eggshells are quickly assimilated into the bird's body.)

Water

Research has shown that birds can go without food more easily than they can go without water. In fact, some birds cannot live for more than 24 hours without water; cockatiels and grassfinches have greater toler-

Feeding and water utensils should be sturdy, although cockatiels are far less destructive than other hookbills! The best types are the various plastic (hook-on) food cups and sealed water containers.

ances for drought, but this does not imply that they should ever be without a daily supply of fresh water. Water is necessary for the transport of food through the digestive system. It softens the food in the crop and acts as a solvent for the enzymes that digest the food. Water also acts as a structural element in the cells and helps to regulate the body temperature. This latter function is very important, as birds do not possess sweat glands, so the excess warmth must be expelled via the lungs and air sacs. A bird that is overheated will also frequently fluff out its feathers to allow cool air between them.

Green Food

The actual needs of all cage and aviary birds, the amount of vitamins and minerals they must have to keep healthy and to keep their plumage in full color, are not fully known. By the same token, the various green foods that we regularly feed to birds have not been sufficiently analyzed to find their content of rarer minerals or to find out how they are related to the minerals found in a bird's feathers. We do know that most green foods contain the more common minerals: iron, copper, zinc, manganese, iodine, calcium, magnesium, potassium, sodium, phosphorus, chlorine, and so on. We also know that it is essential for birds to have access to a small variety of green food every day if they are to remain in the best of health. Each type of green food has a differ-

ent composition of vitamin and minerals; it is also a fact that even green food of a single type, such as lettuce leaves, can vary from one plant to the other! That is why it is so important to give a variety of green food.

It would be ideal if we could obtain our green food from various sources. Unfortunately, most of us who live in the cities have to get our supplies from the local supermarket. It is perhaps possible to grow at least some of your own green food. If you do not have a garden, you may have the possibility of using pots or tubs on the balcony or on a sunny window ledge.

There are special seed mixtures available from pet shops and avicultural suppliers. A large plant trough or a number of tubs and pots will enable you to grow enough green food for the whole year. Chickweed, which is eagerly devoured by many birds, can easily be grown. Germinated bird seed is also good (millet and niger seed germinate quickly), especially when young are being reared.

To germinate seeds, they must not be immersed in water—otherwise they will lose much of their nutritive value—but should be kept just moist. Personally, I have always had good success by washing seed in a kitchen sieve, then spreading it out on damp tea towels or paper towels. As soon as the seeds begin to germinate (usually three or four days), they can be rinsed thoroughly with clean, cold water and then fed to your birds.

All green foods should be washed very thoroughly under a running tap and the water shaken out before it is given to the birds. This by no means will remove every danger, but we will have done our best. Cultivated trees are particularly likely to have been treated and should be used with great caution. Also, avoid collecting weeds near roads as automobile exhausts can deposit toxic substances on them. Wilted green food is dangerous and can lead to disease and death. I therefore advise most strongly that green food be given every day but only in small quantities. I personally do not give more food than can be completely devoured within two hours. Nor do I ever give green food late in the day. Cockatiels should fill their crops with solid (seed) food before retiring for the night.

It is no use feeding large quantities of green food to your birds once or twice a week, as many types of green food act as a laxative. When eaten in quantity, they will give the birds diarrhea. Green food, free of chemical sprays and given daily in conservative amounts, should not have any adverse effects. It is also not necessary to give a great variety of green foods every day—two different types are adequate.

Obtaining green food in the winter is no great problem today. Carrot tops, kale leaves, spinach, lettuce, celery, and parsley are obtainable for most of the year. Grated carrot is an ideal food for all cage birds (and whole carrots are ideal for cockatiels), and small amounts can be mixed with food concentrates or rearing foods. Grated carrot should be used only when fresh; too much of it can also cause diarrhea.

Chickweed is one of the most nutritious green foods available. The birds eat both the half-ripe and ripe seeds as well as the leaves. In all the years I have been an aviculturist, I have never met a breeder who did not have a good word for chickweed. Many give their birds large quantities, although I am personally against this as I have found that too much can cause diarrhea. I am also very conservative with lettuce, spinach, and similar vegetables. Lettuce in particular is one of the most laxative of plants, if given in too large quantities.

Spinach is very rich in vitamins and is particularly beneficial if given together with another green food or seed rich in calcium. Poppy seed and sesame seed are excellent. Spinach and watercress are rich in iron. Carrot tops are much desired and are rich in vitamins. Dandelions are also a favorite green food; both the flowers and the leaves are eaten greedily by birds. In fact, you can safely use the whole plant—flowers, stalks, leaves, and roots. Dandelions are very rich in vitamin A, as are parsley, shepherd's purse, weed and grass seeds, cabbage leaves (the darker the leaves the better), brussels sprouts, and celery. The feeding of the white parts of lettuce or celery is a waste of time. Some birds like freshly mowed (short) grass; others will take the green leaves of cauliflower. Twigs of willow, hazel, and fruit trees can be given regularly. Cockatiels will spend hours chewing them up, with no ill effect. All green food contains a high percentage of protein and carotene while it is still growing; older leaves contain much less protein.

Dried Green Food

Experiments have shown that the nutritional value of dried green food is lower than that of fresh green food, in spite of the modern, technical methods of drying. At present, there are some manufacturers who are producing dried green food especially for the avicultural industry. Such foods are good for emergency use, but of course, cannot replace fresh green food.

Birds That Will Not Eat Green Food

The fresh green food that you offer to your birds each day may be persistently ignored by some of them. To remedy this situation, try the following: A few hours before feeding time, remove all drinking facilities from the cage or aviary. Then, just before feeding, place the green food in water for about five minutes. Then have the wet green food in the cage or aviary. The thirsty birds will go at it to quench their thirsts, probably eating some of the green food in the process. Of course, if the bird(s) still refuse to go at the green food after an hour or so, you should replenish their regular water supply. You may have to carry out this procedure several times before a particular bird realizes what is missing! Once a cockatiel has tasted green food, however, you should have no further difficulties.

Millet sprays **(Panicum and Setaria spp.)** *are the ears of the yellow and white millet, and are greatly enjoyed by both old and young cockatiels throughout the year. When youngsters have just left the nest box millet spray will be found most useful in helping to get them to feed on their own more quickly. Millet sprays are also extremely helpful when training and taming your birds (treats).*

Seeds

Seedeating birds (which include cockatiels) are dependent on various seeds for normal growth, to hold their plumage in top condition, and for reproduction; in short, seed is essential for many birds to stay alive. Diseases and deficiencies are the order of the day in aviaries and cages where birds are supplied with substandard or insufficient seed.

Over the years a great deal of scientific research has gone into finding out which kinds of seeds are most suitable for birds, precisely how much nutritional value there is in each type of seed, which factors can have a good or bad influence on diet, and so on. Seeds contain proteins, vitamins, fats, minerals, carbohydrates, and a little water. Seeds are not a stable "dead" food, but living, breathing organisms. Thus, seeds are good for birds only when they are fresh and unspoiled. Long storage causes seed to spoil.

It is not sound practice to give birds just one or two particular kinds of seed. Feeding them a variety of seeds enables them to develop and maintain their bodies properly.

The most important kinds of seeds for cockatiels include rape, canary grass seed, hemp, rolled oats, millet, sunflower seed, safflower seed, linseed, and niger seed. All these can be mixed together except rape seed, which is best given in a separate feeding dish.

Storing Seeds

If seeds are harvested while unripe, they will quickly spoil or even germinate prematurely. Freshly harvested seeds in good condition should not germinate and should thus have a rest period. The time taken for seeds to develop varies from seed type to seed type. For instance, seeds that are harvested in wet weather are susceptible to mold and bacteria and cannot be stored for long.

Even the best seeds can be damaged or totally spoiled if they are not stored correctly. The biggest dangers for seeds are dampness and high temperatures. At seed-processing plants seeds are stored in cool, well-ventilated, dry premises (if stored in a concrete floored room, it is important to keep containers off the floor by using wooden platforms). If a bird fancier buys a year's supply of seeds and then stores them in warm, damp premises, the nutritive value of the seeds will quickly deteriorate and become useless. After a fairly short time, sometimes just a few months, you can observe that the stored seeds are in no condition to be fed to the birds. It is impossible to state with any degree of accuracy how long most seeds stay in good condition under normal "household" conditions, but as a general rule, seeds that have been kept for more than four months should not be used. Most birdseed is known for its short life. You may have perhaps heard that wheat found in Egyptian pyramids, where it had been placed 3000–4000 years ago, has been germinated so that it actually grew into adult plants! That is total fiction. Such seeds would convert to dust in a fairly short time. Lotus and water lily seeds can live for about 1000 years, however.

Ventilation: Seeds "breathe." They breathe less, according to C. Feyerabend, when they are dormant and dry than they do while developing; however, they must naturally have a constant air supply to remain viable for germination. Seeds will not spoil if kept in a well-sealed container in a cool place for two or three weeks, as long as they are not damp. Damp seeds require more air and the lower layers in a container will die from lack of air.

Frost: Although very dry seeds can withstand frost, it is highly recommended that seed not be kept outside in cold weather, even under a roof. The danger is that the seeds will get damp from rain or snow and be damaged by subsequent frost.

Seeds damaged by frost will germinate, again according to Feyerabend, but they will not develop into fully healthy plants. Such seeds contain less than normal quantities of nutrients. Oil is sometimes added to dead canary grass seed and millet by merchants to give it a shiny and "living" outside appearance. Then they put such seed through a polishing machine. You can frequently smell the rancid odor and feel the oily texture of seeds by running them through your fingers. It is obvious that the suppliers of such seeds should be avoided.

Testing Seed

The bird fancier who questions the quality of bird seed can test it by allowing it to germinate. Not all tests done in this manner are reliable, and a long period of germination does not necessarily mean that the seed is old or stale. But very few bird fanciers have access to a laboratory, so one must make do with the facilities one has. If there is a laboratory in your area, however, it will do no harm to seek advice.

In any case, you can perform a simple test at home: Take a hundred seeds (usually of the same sort), rinse them with clean running water, and dry them with a towel. Lay them on a damp surface (paper towel, for example). Ensure that the seeds are not immersed, as they will lose nutrients and your test will be unreliable. After a few days, most of the seeds should have begun to germinate, and in another three or four days, you should be able to see little shoots emerging from the seeds. The seeds that have thus germinated are easy to count. If, for example, 85 seeds have germinated and 15 have not, you have an 85 percent germination rate. This is a fairly good, not a great, percentage. The best seeds should have a percentage of 90–95 percent, while those with rates lower than 75 percent are rejectable. Seeds with a germination rate of 55–60 percent are totally useless as food for birds and should be destroyed.

It should be noted that hulled oats cannot be germinated in this manner, although theoretically this should be possible. If the hull is carefully removed without damage to the kernel, then even fresh oats can be brought to germination. Too frequently, the seed kernel is damaged and germination cannot take place, although the seed may still have its full nutritive value. Seeds that have a damaged kernel will not keep for very long. Oats do not really have to be dehulled before being fed to hookbilled birds. Your cockatiels are quite capable of dehulling it themselves.

There are various things that can influence the germination process; for example, the color dyes of the nicely decorated paper towel you are using for the germination test!

Most seeds should be kept uniformly moist and must not be permitted to dry out. A good method of doing this is as follows: Take an ordinary soup plate and place a dessert bowl upside down in the center of it. Cut a piece out of a burlap sack to the size of the plate, and place it over the dessert bowl so that the edges hang down into the soup plate. The fibers will "suck up" just enough water to keep the seeds permanently and evenly moist. It is recommended that a second piece of burlap be used to cover the seeds. The edges of this piece must also touch the water. Burlap is porous and allows air through, which is also important for germination.

Germinated or Sprouted Seed

Germinated seeds are extremely good for birds and should never be absent from their diet. In the breeding season, these seeds are especially valuable, and a daily supply of germinated grass and weed seeds should be available to the birds. A regular supply of germinated seeds

Cockatiels love millet spray. It may be soaked in cold water for 24 hours when using it as part of the breeding and rearing foods. Personally, I prefer to offer millet spray dry to avoid any possibility of mold.

make green food less necessary. Sprouted seeds are rich in the enzyme catalase (an enzyme in the blood tissues that brings about the breakdown of hydrogen peroxide into water and oxygen); these seeds are also rich in vitamin A. The germination process uses up some carbohydrates, but the protein content is therefore increased.

It is best to place seeds in a plastic, stainless steel, or chrome container for germination. Galvanized containers should not be used because chemical reactions could affect the seed. If you really do not have anything else, you must paint the interior with a lead-free paint. A regular control is necessary, and

Cockatiels, especially when bored and/or food-satisfied, have the nasty habit of sitting in their food bowl or dish. Smaller cups and closed feeders are therefore preferable for obvious reasons.

ature. The secret of success is in keeping the seeds moist—but not too wet!

The Most Important Seeds

In the wild, each bird is its own master, fulfilling its own nutritional requirements. Thus it is understandable that commercial birdseed mixtures, with their fixed percentages of different seeds, are not always the answer to satisfying your birds' needs. I am a great believer in the use of various seeds given in automatic seed dispensers, which are available in various models from avicultural suppliers. Each kind of seed can then be made available in a separate dispenser so that you will be able to control quantities and your birds will be able to eat what they want. You'll need only three or four dispensers, which will soon pay for themselves by eliminating the waste of seeds that the birds do not need at a particular time. You can also make your own dispensers, but do not use plywood. The sheets can separate after a time, forming ideal hiding places for all sorts of unpleasant organisms.

One disadvantage of an automatic seed dispenser is that it may easily become blocked. Regular control checks are therefore essential. Place the dispensers in the covered part of the aviary or in a light part of the night shelter. It's a good

each galvanized can should be repainted annually. The containers in which sprouted seeds are given to the birds must be first thoroughly washed with boiling water and a stiff scrubbing brush.

The seeds must not lay in heaps, but should be spread thinly over the whole surface so that each individual seed remains in contact with the air as well as the damp sacking or paper towels. Sacking (burlap) must first be boiled to kill any disease organisms. The seeds should be rinsed with lukewarm water frequently during the process and kept moist (not wet) with a house plant watering device that has not been used with artificial fertilizer. The container must be placed in a light, airy spot, out of any extremes of temper-

idea to provide some extra seed containers, perhaps two in the covered flight and one in the night shelter. There is nothing more stressful to a group of birds than to have to fight over the food containers. The stronger birds will usually stick together, leaving the weaker birds with a shortage of food. In most cases ensure that the birds you keep in groups are compatible with each other and keep an eye on them (but do not automatically assume that a resting bird is being kept away from the food.) You must consider that each bird is an individual and does not always conform to everything you may read in books. This is good; it makes your hobby all the more interesting!

Oil- and Fat-rich Seeds

Hemp *(Cannabis sativa):* It is well known that hemp has a stimulatory effect on the reproductive system. A relative of marijuana, hemp is a very oily seed that should be given to the birds very conservatively. Overfeeding can lead to liver problems or the hens' going to lay too early in the season. (These eggs will be fertile as the resident cocks will also have been stimulated by the hemp.) It is important to give hemp at the correct times, then, and in small quantities—say half a teaspoon per bird in the late mornings. Hemp can be strewn over the aviary floor; you have no need to worry that it will be ignored!

Hemp is an excellent "pick-me-up" or tonic, especially during the cold winter days. Whenever the temperature falls below freezing, I give my birds extra hemp in their rations. Hemp is low in carbohydrates (approximately 18 percent), but protein and fat content are high (approximately 19 percent and 32 percent, respectively). Important minerals, especially calcium and phosphorus, are present, as well as amino acids such as lysine, methionine, and cystine—excellent for feather development and growth— and tyrosine (essential for the good health and functioning of the thyroid gland).

Linseed or Flax *(Linum usitatissimum):* Flax seed is cultivated for its oil content and for the fibrous nature of the stems (from which linen is manufactured); it is also high in digestible carbohydrates. The seed husk contains a substance that causes the seed to expand if it comes into contact with warm water. Such seed is good for young or sick birds. Moreover, it contains the anti-vitamin B6 factor linatine, which has the character of an antibiotic. Personally, I find linseed very important for cockatiels (and other pet birds), though it should not be given in large quantities. Canary breeders give plenty of linseed to their birds in order to improve the shine of the plumage (it works with cockatiels as well). Linseed is especially useful during the molt, and I have found it to be excellent in promoting a trouble-free, complete change of plumage. Unlike budgies, cockatiels will usually eat linseed.

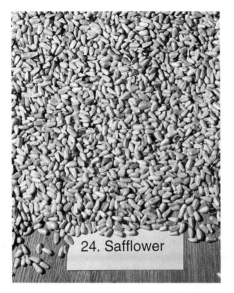

24. Safflower

1. Medium Striped Sunflower

17. White Sunflowers (Calif.)

Safflower and sunflower seeds should only be part of the cockatiel's seed diet. Due to their sweet taste, sunflowers are very well-liked and most birds become easily addicted to them. Since sunflowers don't contain much lysine (a protein essential for feather formation and growth) the birds should not be allowed to make sunflowers their main food source.

But remember, give it only in small quantities.

Niger Seed *(Guizota oleifera):* Niger seed is grown primarily for its oil in many parts of the world, but especially along the valley of the river Niger in Africa, where there are many large plantations. These seeds are especially appreciated by birds in the fall and winter, but they must also be available to the hens in the spring, prior to the breeding season. Many fanciers withdraw the supply of niger seed from the diet after laying is completed.

These seeds are high in protein (approximately 21 percent) and fat (approximately 40 percent); there is ample carbohydrate (13 percent), too, and almost 4 percent minerals; calcium and potassium content are also high. It is important always to buy fresh, shiny niger seed in small quantities. Owing to their high oil content, these seeds can quickly become rancid if damaged or spoiled. It is reported that niger seed contains many essential amino acids including lysine, cystine, tyrosine, and methionine.

Rape Seed (*Brassica* spp.): This small seed is cultivated in many parts of the world. In Europe, it is mainly grown in Denmark; in the United States, one is mainly dependent on imports from Canada. The variety grown in Indonesia is poorer in carbohydrates but richer in fiber. *Brassica dichtoma* and *B. glauca* rape seeds are the two most important varieties. I believe that rape seed should be fed to cockatiels more than is the usual practice today. When it is first offered, the birds may hesitate, but they will soon accept it gratefully. Rape seed contains approximately 19 percent carbohydrates, 20 percent protein, 50 percent fat, 4 percent minerals, and 7.5 percent moisture. These seeds have a calcium and potassium content and should be used especially during the breeding and molting periods.

Safflower Seed *(Carthamus tinctorius):* Like sunflower seed, safflower seed is fairly poor in tyrosine, lysine, methionine, and cystine. However, it contains important amounts of protein (approximately 14 percent), fat (28 percent), carbohydrates (16 percent), and some minerals (5 percent). In England and on the Continent, fanciers seldom give this somewhat bitter-tasting seed to their birds, and in my experi-

ence, I have found that most cockatiels are not particularly fond of it. In fact, it takes up to five months for cockatiels used to sunflower seed (which has a smaller nutritive value) to begin to take safflower seed. It is therefore strange that, in the United States, safflower seed is regarded as an extremely important seed and is given regularly and in quantity to cockatiels and other hookbills. In spite of this, I have found that cockatiels do not become attached to it, much preferring the sweet-tasting sunflower seed.

Sunflower Seed *(Helianthus annus):* Although sunflower seed is regarded by many aviculturists as essential parrot seed, there is a danger that the birds will like the taste of it so much that they will neglect or even ignore all the other seeds they are given. You must therefore take steps to ensure that your cockatiels make full use of all of their rations. Sunflower seed contains approximately 25 percent raw protein and 45 percent raw fat. Unfortunately, it contains very little carbohydrate and very little lysine in the protein. (Lysine is essential for the growth and development of plumage.)

There are four main varieties of sunflower seeds: dark (small), white (small), narrow-striped (medium), and broad-striped (large). As the fat and protein content is easily digestible, sunflower seed is highly nutritious for sick birds and for birds in fall and winter. Other kinds of seeds must also be given, however; birds that are given an exclusive diet of sunflower seed will not survive.

Sunflower seed is rich in vitamin A but low in cyanocobalamin (B12), D3, E, and K vitamins. Thiamine (B1), riboflavin (B2), niacin (B3), pantothenic acid (B5), and pyridoxine (B6) are contained in only small quantities. The mineral content includes adequate iron and potassium, some manganese and phosphorus, and traces of calcium, copper, and some others. The protein (especially in dehulled sunflower seed) is high in 12 amino acids, including methionine, crystine, and tyrosine. This is important because protein is always required in large quantities for growth, plumage, and egg production. A deficiency could result in a difficult and incomplete molt, for example, or feather plucking as the bird will eat its own feathers to obtain protein.

Starchy Seeds

Canary Grass Seed or White Seed (Phalaris canariensis): This well-known seed is eaten greedily and in large quantities by cockatiels. Unfortunately, the seed is variable in quality, depending on where it is cultivated. The best quality is the Mazagan Grass Seed, which, together with the Spanish seed, is most often used in seed mixtures. The seed cultivated in Morocco, Turkey, Argentina, and Australia is of somewhat inferior quality. Spanish grass seed is the largest in size. Canary grass seed contains a high percentage of carbohydrate, but fat is very low (56 percent and 4 percent, respectively).

The protein content is about 14 percent. The seed is low in lysine and lacks cystine altogether.

Millet Seed (Panicum spp. and Setaria spp.): These relatively small, round seeds are an essential part of seed mixtures for cage and aviary birds; cockatiels eat them eagerly and in large quantities. There are various kinds that more or less resemble each other. They are poor in lycine but rich in leucine. Many birdkeepers raise their own white millet (Panicum miliaceum), which grows well in poor soils and with little rain. The plants reach 12 feet in height! The "real" millet sprays (Setaria viride) are available in pet stores. These should not be omitted from any cage or aviary; cockatiels are mad about them! There are, among others, white, yellow, red, and Japanese millets. Senegal millet is very small-grained, unlike Japanese millet, and is thus suitable for small tropical finches, but it is also greedily devoured by cockatiels. Most millet seeds contain approximately 60 percent carbohydrates, 12 percent protein, 4 percent fat, and 4 percent minerals. The essential amino acids, lysine, methionine, and cystine, as well as tyrosine, are contained in useful amounts.

Oats (Avena sativa): After removal of the hulls, oats are called groats. I give these seeds to my birds especially in the fall and winter. Oats are rich in arginine, vitamin E, vitamins B1, B2, and B6, calcium, potassium, tyrosine, methionine, cystine, and lysine. The carbohydrate content of oats is approximately 64 percent, protein 14 percent, and fat 8 percent. Owing to their absorbent nature, groats are useful for administering fluid vitamins, pure cod-liver oil, or medicines to the birds. Whole oats can be used for germination, during which the enzyme diastase is produced.

Rearing Food

The first four to five weeks in a cockatiel's life are the most crucial. Most seed-eating birds hatch from the egg in a relatively early stage of development. It should go without saying that during this time of growth and development of the body as well as a feathery coat, it is imperative that the hatchlings receive a rich and diverse supply of food.

Seed-eating wild birds, including cockatiels rearing young, will forage for large numbers of insects as well as the seeds, leaves, grasses, and fruits to make up a diet often much more varied than they receive in cage and aviary. However, there are many rearing diets available under a number of brand names that provide varied and healthful nutrition to domestic birds. A rich choice is especially available for the canary breeder (such rearing foods can also be given to cockatiels and other kinds of birds with no worries). It is a fact that similar percentages of amino acids, fats, carbohydrates, vitamins, and minerals are required by all young birds. Thus, rearing

Watch for over-feeding! It is clear that these birds are bored and have had more then their fill, and perch now in their food bowl. Therefore, do like most aviculturists and feed your birds only twice a day (morning and evening) for just a couple of hours.

foods that contain these necessary ingredients will normally produce healthy youngsters. Unfortunately, however, many of these rearing foods contain by-products that are not necessarily accepted by all birds. It is therefore important to give your birds a choice of two or three kinds of rearing food, thus allowing them to choose what they find best for their nestlings.

Concentrated or Universal Food

Concentrated food is especially important to adult birds. It is available on the market under various brand names. It is best to use only well-known brands, which are always scientifically prepared and tested. Concentrated foods contain items that may not be available in a normal seed mixture. Most commercial seed mixtures are deficient in amino acids (arginine, lysine, and methionine), provitamin A, choline, and riboflavin. Seeds do not contain vitamin D3, but it is contained in the animal product element of concentrated food. Providing a good brand of concentrated food to your birds is therefore a high priority if you are to maintain them in top condition. It must be used all year round, not just in the breeding and molting seasons, and given daily in small quantities. I say "small quantities" because, in warm weather, it can quickly spoil and could become dangerous.

Insects

Cockatiels and other seed-eating birds also make use of insects in their diets. This is especially the case when young are being reared in the nest; the nestlings thus receive an important portion of animal protein in their diet. Even adult seedeaters are not averse to eating the odd spider, fly, worm, or anything they can overpower.

Suitable insect (and other invertebrate) foods include ants' "eggs" (really pupae), spiders, flies, tubifex, waterfleas, small mealworms, whiteworms *(Enchytraeus),* crickets,

grasshoppers, beetles, fruit flies, and wax moths.

Fruit

Fruit should be available to birds at all times. In addition to a piece of banana or a halved orange, you can use seedless raisins, sweet apples, and pears. Other fruits you can try on your birds include currants, strawberries, apricots, fresh pineapples, papaya, blackberries, lemons, dates (without the pit), raspberries, grapefruits, juniper berries, cherries, gooseberries, rowan berries, mandarins, melons, peaches, plums, rose hips, hawthorn berries (remove the thorns from the twigs), wild elder (though the juice may stain the birds' plumage), and figs.

Remember that the berries of the dwarf elder *(Sambucus ebulus)* are poisonous. Also, poisonous plants such as golden rain or laburnum (especially the seeds), yew, the bark of the silver birch *(Betula pendula),* ivy, and black and fly honeysuckle *(Lonicera nigra* and *L. xylosteum)* should never be given to cockatiels. The wild honeysuckle *(L. pericylmenum),* however, is enjoyed by cockatiels.

Table Scraps

In this chapter, I have tried to explain how and why it is important that birds receive a varied, balanced diet. Such a diet should not include table scraps. The starches and fats in such foods as potatoes and butter are not suited to cockatiels. Cakes, candies, and other sweetmeats should also be kept out of your birds' reach. The habit of allowing tame cockatiels to "eat at the table" should be discouraged. When you are dining, leave the bird in its cage and give it a piece of brown bread or a bit of cheese. To keep a bird healthy and fit, do not feed it table scraps!

Bird Pellets/ Extruded Diets

No matter how hard you try, you cannot give your cockatiels the type or great variety of food they would find in their natural habitat. Birds in cages and aviaries should therefore be given a menu that is as high as possible in quality and variety. The great growth in the popularity of aviculture in the last decade has brought about increased activity in the animal food industry. All kinds of food are available in the pet shops and other outlets, sometimes making a choice very difficult. In the last few years, "easy-to-feed" extruded diets and pelleted diets have become very popular. These types of diets can be placed in clean feeders or dispensers, and the birds can eat when and as they choose.

Extruded diets are not new to the pet industry, but they are the newest diet alternative for pet birds. They look similar to standard pelleted diets, but looks are deceiving. In the pelleting process, dry ground-up nutrients are compressed into a pellet, which is heated to 190°F (88°C). During extrusion, wet ingredients are combined into a soupy mixture that is subjected to approximately 25 different atmospheric pressures and temperatures up to 320°F (179°C). A pellet's inner core becomes insulated during compression and does not reach 171°F (77°C), the temperature needed to kill salmonella and pseudomonas viruses. Extrusion, however, is the most bacteriologically safe method of formulating a diet, and it makes the food the most digestible for the end user. The wet process also allows manufacturers to form different shapes and textures that appeal to a bird's natural curiosity and make the diet more readily acceptable. Because the ingredients are already broken down, extruded diets offer greater digestibility.

Obviously, a cockatiel or any other bird that has spent its whole life feeding on a diet consisting largely of seeds is not likely to become suddenly enthusiastic about extruded diets and/or pellets. Converting a bird to such a change in diet can sometimes be a difficult task and may require much patience. The best method is to give the birds a 50/50 mixture of seeds and extruded diet or pellets for a couple of weeks, then over the next month gradually increase the quantity of pellets and decrease the

The number of cockatiels kept purely as house pets is increasing steadily. People of all walks of life are discovering that these charming, attractive birds are very easy to stand and hand- or finger-tame. There is an occasional brilliant linguist among them, too!

quantity of seeds. Personally, I think cockatiels should always have access to fresh green food, seeds, and fruit as well as pellets or extruded diets.

Cleanliness and Hygiene

To prevent the spread of disease, all utensils used in the feeding of your birds should be kept scrupulously clean. Many birdkeepers believe that sick birds do not require any food or water; this is nonsense! It does no harm for the patient to eat. Indeed, give the bird its favorite food. In addition, a sick bird kept in heated accommodation is likely to

become very thirsty. To prevent dehydration, it is very important to have a supply of clean, fresh water at all times. Moreover, you can use the water to administer medicines and extra vitamins.

Utensils should be cleaned daily, preferably in the morning. The empty hulls should be blown off the seed before refilling the containers. Many beginners make the mistake of putting new seed on top of the old, hulls and all. Many an apparently full dish contains little other than empty hulls. Personally, I spread all the seed daily out on a sheet of newspaper, then blow the hulls away. By doing this I eliminate the risk that the lower layer of seeds is never used and gets gradually old, forming an ideal breeding ground for bacteria and pests.

Food vessels should be cleaned regularly, and food and water containers from cages and aviaries should be cleaned and disinfected at least once a week. Do not return seeds to containers that are anything but bone dry. Damp seeds will soon turn moldy and become infected with bacteria and other organisms that can endanger the birds' health.

Conclusion

You can ensure that your birds are not deficient in any dietary constituent by using the following menu:

1. A good seed mixture, with a large variety of seeds. There are excellent seed mixtures for cockatiels on the market. A good mixture is the staple part of the diet. Mix your seed mixture with a good brand of extruded diet or pellets.

2. A good brand of concentrated food. Most products on the market are of excellent quality, so it is not necessary to make your own. But it is important that your cockatiels receive a supplement of animal protein; they cannot thrive without it!

3. Fresh fruit without rotting parts and fresh, unblemished green food. These foods contain many vitamins and minerals. I would also include many kinds of wild plants and berries.

4. Fresh, unblemished twigs. These are not only good to supplement the diet, they also provide the birds with exercise and recreation. Twigs of willow, privet, and fruit trees are ideal.

5. A supply of gravel or other insoluble grit to grind the food in the stomach.

6. Soluble grit, mainly as a supply of calcium. Watch out for the charcoal that is sometimes mixed in with commercial bird grit. Birds do not digest charcoal; it remains in their bodies for a time, and because charcoal is highly absorbent, it soaks up important nutrients from the gut, including certain vitamins.

7. Bathing and drinking water. In freezing weather, drinking water can turn to ice. This process can be inhibited (but not altogether avoided) by dissolving glucose (one tablespoon per pint) in the water.

Chapter Four

Taming and Training

There are many opinions as to what kind of bird is best for taming and training. Long experience has convinced me that most of these theories are nonsense. For instance, some people think that a bird's color and markings are of prime importance. Some birds do indeed learn better and more quickly than others, but there is no evidence that the outward appearance of the bird has anything whatsoever to do with its intelligence. Another myth is that only cock birds can learn to repeat words, but I have known hens with a vocabulary that would be the envy of any cock. On the other hand, age is an important factor. If you want a cockatiel to learn to talk (and not all cockatiels will), you must start with a young bird, which is more "open to suggestion" and more eager to endear itself to its trainer than an older bird. Such a bird must be separated from its brothers and sisters—indeed, from any other birds—so that it can become a member of the family and thus learn to speak, rather than to imitate the sounds of its fellow birds. If a cockatiel is isolated from all dis-tractions, it will be much more likely to become tame and attentive toward its trainer—and this is your initial objective.

The First Steps

As mentioned earlier, the most stressful time for a pet cockatiel is the first few days in its new home. It is therefore important that the bird be quickly reassured that it is not going to come to any harm. On placing a cockatiel in its new cage, you should leave it to its own devices for the rest of that day and night. Thereafter, however, do not allow the bird too much peace and quiet. If it is to be successfully tamed and trained, the sooner you start, the better. Put your hand in the cage and hold it there. (It is best initially to wear a strong canvas or leather glove; a cockatiel's beak and claws are amazingly sharp and strong!) The bird will soon accept your hand as part of the cage "furniture," especially if you move your hand up and down. I have more than once suc-ceeded in getting a young budgerigar or cockatiel to sit on my finger within 15 minutes of the start of its first training session.

It is important that the bird gets to know you intimately. Thus, each time you bring food or water, clean the cage, or are in any other way occupied with the bird, call it by its name clearly. A short, easily repeated name such as Bobby, Jack, Ann, or Kathy is preferable.

When the bird realizes that your hand does not present a danger, it will soon accept the hand as a "normal" part of the cage fittings. Some birds will take longer to do this than others; it is a matter of individuality. On no account should you lose patience and make sudden movements; you may thus sacrifice any progress you have made so far. Once the bird shows little or no fear of your hand, you can stretch out the forefinger and gently stroke the bird's breast and lower abdomen, gradually working your finger toward its feet. When you gently press the lower abdomen, just above the feet, the bird should then transfer itself to your finger, using it as a perch. If this does not succeed at first, return to the first part of the exercise and give the bird more time to get used to your hand. After your hand is once more accepted without fear, try once more to get the bird to perch on your finger.

If the bird starts fluttering wildly about during your efforts, continue to hold your hand in the cage without movement until it settles down. On no account should you remove your hand, as the bird may get the idea (as far as a bird is capable) that it has "scored a victory" and thus be more than likely to repeat the action next time. Do not withdraw your hand from the cage until some progress, however small it may be, has been achieved.

Outside the Cage

As soon as the bird accepts your finger as a perch without panicking, you must teach it to go back onto its perch from your finger. This can be accomplished by holding your finger next to the perch and making a slight encouraging movement; at the same time, a word of command like *"Up"* can be used. Continue this for several days until the bird is thoroughly familiar with when it should

Interaction is very important. Tame birds should be dealt with on a daily basis for several hours at a time.

Cockatiels, both cocks and hens (the bird in the picture is a female), will make affectionate pets. Both sexes are quite intelligent and (I believe) equally easy to train and tame.

of similar dimensions, in order to recover the bird.

If you press the perch gently against its abdomen, the bird will usually climb onto it. Then slowly move the stick and bird passenger back to the cage and hold it next to the open door, at which point the bird will most likely climb back into the cage without further fuss. However, it is important to persist with this training until the bird returns to its cage on command. If you have to catch the bird every time you want it to go back in its cage, the experience will be not only unpleasant and possibly stressful for the bird, but it will also leave you with an unsatisfied feeling.

You can also use a perch instead of the finger method described above when training the bird to come out of its cage. Place the T perch in the cage (via the detachable cage bottom if it won't fit through the door) and leave it for the bird to get accustomed to it. Then slowly pick up the perch and move it about, repeating the movement several times until the bird accepts it as a natural phenomenon. Sometimes a bird may react more positively if you approach it from behind, moving the T perch across the back and head in a semicircular motion until it reaches the lower abdomen. Then gently press the bird and encourage it to step onto the perch. If it does not immediately step onto the perch, use increasing upward pressure until it is literally "forced" to move onto the perch. If the bird should start

sit on your finger and when it should return to its perch.

A cockatiel's first trip outside the cage must be short. First, get the bird to sit on your finger, then gently withdraw your hand through the cage door, all the time talking to the bird in a reassuring voice. The first time it is out of the cage, it will want to fly around and inspect every corner of the room. With good training, a cockatiel will return to its cage on command. At first, however, it may have to be lured back by the prospect of a food reward, but later these treats should not be necessary. It is recommended that you use a fixed command, such as *"Come."* If the bird does not obey, you may have to resort to using a thin bamboo stick about half an inch in diameter, or a T-shaped perch

getting jumpy and obviously nervous, wait a few minutes for it to calm down before proceeding; otherwise it may start scrambling and fluttering about the cage, perhaps even developing a strong fear of the T perch.

It will not take a bird long to discover parts of the room that are its favorite spots, often close to mirrors, windows, and other shiny objects. Make a note of these places so that you can keep a good eye on your bird when it's out of the cage. When you think of it, letting a cockatiel fly freely around a room can be a risky business. With its considerable wingspan and the presence of fragile objects in the room, the bird could cause damage to your property or even injury to itself if you do not take adequate precautions (refer to the Table of Dangers on page 50).

After the bird has become accustomed to the room and is able to return to its cage without difficulties on command, you can proceed with further training—such as getting it to move from one hand to the other. Allow the bird to transfer from one hand to the other, by jumping or stepping, as much as it wants. This can be a very pleasurable and relaxing activity for both you and the bird. When the cockatiel grows accustomed to such activities and realizes that you pose no danger, it will begin exploring other parts of your body; running up your arm, sitting on your shoulder or head, nibbling gently on your ear, tugging at a lock of your hair, or "talking to you."

Cockatiels are easily tamed and may soon learn to imitate the human voice.

Now you can really say that you are the proud owner of a hand-tamed cockatiel.

T Perch Training

As mentioned before, a T perch can be used for persuading a "difficult" student to return to its cage after the lesson is over. A T-shaped perch resembles a natural resting place and can be used for many aspects of training. Although many bird trainers use their finger in initial training, others prefer to use a T perch. Such a perch should have a rough surface so that the bird can get a good grip. If a perch is too smooth, it should be abraded with coarse sandpaper, but take care not to leave sharp splinters behind.

Before proceeding, it should be pointed out that birds cannot tell the sex of another bird by its appearance. It is behavior that enables them to recognize male from female; take, for example, the aggressiveness of males as they look at each other. When a hen looks at a male, however, she will often slant her head to one side and look away, as though she had no interest whatsoever. If aroused, though, she may watch him closely while making nodding and bowing movements and perhaps fanning her tail out, all the while making little grinding sounds with her beak.

All this is by way of saying that you must always approach your bird with care and understanding. Any object—be it finger, hand, or T perch—that is moved directly toward a bird may be seen as a possible aggressive movement by a male cockatiel. The T perch should be moved toward the bird from the side very, very slowly. If your timing is right, the bird will perceive the perch at the last possible moment—too late to take evasive action! You then press the perch softly against its abdomen, near its feet. But if the bird perceives your movements before you are ready, move the perch slowly away and hold it behind your back for a while. When the bird relaxes, start again, perhaps moving even more slowly than on your first attempt. It is not necessary to move back to the far corner of the room. Start again each time from the position you were already in at each attempt. Patience, kindness, and repetition are the key words that will

result in success in this as in all other kinds of training.

Remember to keep talking gently and reassuringly to your bird all the time you are training it. What you say does not really matter, as long as you say something! The human voice, used in the correct manner, will inspire trust and have a calming effect. On no account should you scold or shout at the bird with an aggressive attitude during training; this will only make your task all the more difficult.

The initial training of a cockatiel will take up quite a bit of time and can be very tiresome for the trainer. However, if it is your goal to have a tame bird, giving up is out of the question; you must ensure that some progress, however little, is made at each training session. Otherwise, further training will become difficult, tedious, and frustrating for the trainer and distressing to the bird.

The Ladder

After the initial training, which may take few or many lessons depending on the individuality of the bird, you can proceed to teaching it other tricks. When the bird is outside the cage, teach it to move from one hand to the other, from hand to T perch and vice versa, or from T perch to T perch. Always talk to it and praise it lavishly when it does what you want. Personally, I like to let a bird step just once or twice on my finger (or hand) or T perch, before placing it back in its cage (which it will regard as a sort of "safe haven").

Whenever your bird has learned something new, however simple, it will be enthusiastic, even though this may not be immediately apparent. To calm the bird down, it should be allowed to rest in its cage for half an hour or so before beginning again. This time you can let the bird step back and forth four or five times. When perched on your hand or on the T perch, it will often look inquisitively around the room, maybe even flying off to explore. There is no harm in this, of course, and if you have carried out the training correctly, you should have no difficulty in getting the bird back onto your finger or T perch or into its cage.

Once the bird is accustomed to moving from hand to hand and back into its cage, the moment has arrived to walk slowly around the room with the bird perched pertly on either hand, finger, or perch, all the while talking to it reassuringly. Once this has been successfully accomplished, return it to the cage for half an hour or so; then try again. To give the bird more confidence, try holding it (on hand, finger, or perch) a little above your head. A bird likes to perch as high up as possible; it feels more secure up there. The proximity of your voice may make it a little uneasy at first, but it will soon get used to the sound.

When using a second perch, coax the bird to step from one to the other by gentle pressure on its

Head scratching is one of the nicest actions you can treat your bird with and is one of the most important bonding behavior traits among pairs!

abdomen in the familiar way. Start imitating a staircase by holding one hand a little lower than the other. As soon as the bird changes hands, move the first hand above the second, and so on, so that it moves as if climbing a ladder. Soon you will be able to get it to go "up" or "down" your ladder as you wish. When you first try this, the new pupil will probably become a little confused and start flying about. In such a case, calmly return it to its cage and try again later; you will succeed in due course. If the bird gets very nervous and perhaps flutters to the floor, approach it slowly and offer your finger, hand, or T perch. Do not rush anything and speak reassuringly at all times. If the bird runs or flies away, let it calm down and take stock of its surroundings before trying again. If you find it necessary to catch a nervous bird quickly for any

For training as a tame, talking pet, it is advisable that a young healthy bird be selected and taken away from the care of its parents as soon as it is seen to be feeding entirely on its own.

reason, use a towel, sweater, or similar article to throw over it. Do not use your bare hand to catch a nervous cockatiel; it will bite, and a cockatiel's bite can be extremely painful!

If you must restrain a cockatiel in your hand, allow its back to rest against the palm of your hand. The bird's head should be restrained by gently holding your thumb and middle finger around its neck, with your index finger on top of its head, like a "helmet." Place your ring finger around its abdomen, and your little finger resting behind its legs or in line with its tail.

Once the bird has learned these initial lessons, you will not find it too difficult to introduce the "ladder" trick. I have discovered that things are somewhat easier for the bird if it practices the exercises in front of a large mirror. After getting over the shock of seeing "another" cockatiel, it will soon want to show off and try to impress its reflection. In some cases the bird actually falls in love with itself. Nothing is wrong with that, of course, provided you continue to give the bird your attention and leave it alone during its romantic spells.

The training of cockatiels and many other bird species is not difficult as long as it is done with devotion and understanding. As the human teacher is often regarded as a mother/father and as the bird's behavioral pattern dictates that a large part of its "education" consists of copying set examples, it is not at all difficult for a young cockatiel to learn certain tricks and games.

A cockatiel must always have special attention from its owner and should never be left to spend its entire life in solitary confinement in a cage. A single trained bird needs a great deal of your attention every day. Tame and untrained birds may be kept together, but if you have any untamed birds, keep them away from those that have been trained. A trained bird will soon take on the "bad habits" of its untamed friends and forget much of what you have taught it. Personally, I find it preferable to keep all trained birds separate, although this is not absolutely necessary. Of course, you can allow trained birds to "perform" as a group, but as soon as the show is over, you should separate them again from each other so that they don't take over each other's unique ways of performing tricks. Fundamentally, there is nothing wrong with this group activity, but there is a chance that individual birds will lose their "loyalty" toward their keeper. Hand-reared cockatiels, which have depended on a human keeper virtually from birth, are of course easiest to train. But young birds are generally amenable, no matter how they have been raised. Older birds can be trained, too, but it requires more time, dedication, and patience.

Tricks

Most of us have heard, at some time during our education, that all animals learn through the process of association. The Russian physiologist Ivan Petrovitch Pavlov (1849–1936) demonstrated this in his experiments with dogs. Each time the dogs were fed, a bell was sounded. After a little time, the dogs would start salivating each time they heard the bell without being fed. In other words, the dogs had learned to associate the sound of the bell with being fed. For cockatiel training, this process of association can be very useful indeed. If the bird is rewarded each time it does well, it will associate the thing it has done well with the pleasurable reward. In other words, it will realize the reward is a consequence of its action (especially tricks involving a cockatiel's natural behavior, including jumping, dancing, and hanging by its beak. Tricks using large props, such as a wagon, may be frightening to a cockatiel).

What sort of a reward should be offered? I have found millet spray to be a sensible choice. It is delicious to cockatiels, and they never seem to tire of it.

Occasionally, a bird may get "bored" during training or when performing, as though its mind is "miles away" and its whole attention is not being applied to the subject at hand. A good way of regaining the bird's undivided attention is to use a "cricket," one of those common toys that makes a clicking sound when the metal tongue is depressed. The sharp tone of the clicks will soon

This white face pearl cockatiel is waiting for its next training session. It is a myth that color mutations are unfit to be trained.

rekindle the bird's interest in the "game," after which, of course, it is appropriate to present a reward of a few seeds.

No Food

Another method worth trying is to remove the food hoppers from the bird's cage a couple of hours before each training session (but don't let it go any longer without food). Once your bird is hand-tamed, you can try hand-feeding it. First offer it some millet or other tasty seeds, then click the cricket as soon as the bird accepts them. Then, each time you give your bird a special treat, make the same clicking sound. Soon it will associate the sound with the food it enjoys so much.

As to the kinds of tricks you may want to teach your bird, there are

It does not hurt a bird to have its wing feathers clipped, and after the next molt the clipped feathers will be replaced by new ones. It is advisable to ask an avian veterinarian or an experienced aviculturist to do this task, or show you exactly how to do it yourself.

many possibilities. Sometimes the bird will discover or even invent its own tricks or games. For example, Freddie, one of my cockatiels, clearly enjoyed taking a coin from my desk and dropping it into an empty ashtray. Then he would return to another coin, repeating the process until there were no coins left. Next, Freddie would carry all the coins to the edge of the desk and drop them on the floor. Having achieved this, he would fly to the floor, retrieve each coin, and return them one by one to the ashtray. After Freddie had done this twice— to the great delight of my little daughter—I would reward him with a few seeds (usually millet) in the ashtray, then summon him with a click of my cricket to take a well-earned rest. When Freddie tired of the game, he would come, pleased as punch, to sit on my head or shoulder!

Wing Clipping

Many bird trainers clip the wing feathers of a bird to prevent it from flying around the room while training is in progress. Personally, I do not have a strong opinion on this matter. I have trained birds with clipped wings as well as birds in their natural state, and I honestly cannot say which birds were easier to work with. Of course, if the wings of a bird that is not yet tame are clipped, you won't have to chase it too far if it leaves the T perch. However, another very important fact to remember is that a cockatiel with radically clipped wings will not be able to escape should it encounter a cat or other predatory animal!

If a bird is treated in a calm and controlled manner, however, and you take adequate precautions to prevent its leaving the room when it is out of its cage, wing clipping will not make much difference one way or the other. In the final analysis, the decision for or against may depend on the temperament of the individual bird (especially in the case of an older one). You might start training without clipping the bird's wings. Then, if you find your pupil is rather obstinate, clipping a few flight feathers might be a good idea.

If you find clipping desirable, it should be performed on both wings, so that the bird is unable to fly. Use a sharp pair of scissors and clip off all but the two outermost flight feathers and seven of the secondary feathers of each wing as near to the base as possible. Take great care not to cut the feathers too short, as this can cause bleeding. It does not hurt a bird to have its feathers clipped, and after the next molt, the clipped feathers will be replaced by new ones. Thus, if the bird is not fully trained by this time, another clipping will be necessary.

Note: Never assume that a cockatiel with clipped wings cannot escape if a door or window is left open. Lost-and-found ads are filled with plaintive reminders of this every summer.

Wing clipping. Use a sharp pair of scissors and clip off all but the two outermost flight and six or seven of the secondary feathers of each wing as near to the base as possible. If you are inexperienced, work with an assistant and wear leather gloves; or, better still, entrust the job to your veterinarian.

The Talking Cockatiel

Once a cockatiel has been trained to come to hand, one can really concentrate on giving it speech lessons. Many fanciers are of the opinion that a cockatiel can be tamed and taught to speak at the same time, but I think it better for the bird to be hand-tamed before speech lessons begin. Later in this section, I describe a method of simultaneous training, for those who want to try it. Not every cockatiel is a gifted student; it depends entirely on the individual. In comparison with many parrots, which can easily pick up 100 or more words, cockatiels can learn only a limited number of words and expressions, though they are quite capable of learning to whistle tunes. Although young birds usually make the best pupils, it is not impossible to train a bird that is a few years old, provided the trainer has the necessary enthusiasm and patience.

Before embarking on speech lessons, a bird must be completely at ease with its trainer. A new arrival should always be placed close to people, but not so close that it will become frightened. Once the lessons begin, distractions—such as children playing noisily, dogs barking, music playing loudly—must be kept out of sight and hearing. Should your bird be frightened during its first few days of training, only patience and kindness can win back its trust and regain its undivided

Once a cockatiel has been trained to come to hand, one can really concentrate on giving it speech lessons.

attention for the words and phrases you may wish to teach him. This cannot be done in a few days; it may mean several weeks of hard work! To make the bird trust and love you, you must give it your constant attention. If you cannot or will not do this, then you cannot expect to be very successful in training and teaching your bird to talk. A bird that is only given its daily ration of food and water and is otherwise left to its own devices will never become tame and will, of course, never learn to repeat words.

Intelligence

Most readers of this book are aware that animals learn only by imitation and/or repetition. Birds, including cockatiels, cannot reason or think in the sense we understand, though some birds give a pretty good impression of being able to do just that! A cockatiel should therefore be taught to repeat or to imitate things that have attracted its attention. The repetition of certain sentences and the answers to certain questions should be taught so that they are used at the appropriate times (see page 89).

Male or Female

I firmly believe that it does not matter whether the bird to be trained is male or female. In spite of the common belief that the male is easier to train, I have found that both sexes are equally capable of learning to perform tricks and to repeat words and sentences. Of course, you are going to find the occasional "dunce" of either sex. I have observed several times that the best-trained birds are simply the trainers' favorite pupils, whether male or female. Indeed, I doubt if many trainers know or even care what sex their birds are. Of course, this attitude is different as far as the breeders are concerned; for obvious reasons it is essential that they know the sexes of their birds.

One point worth mentioning here is that children and women make the best speech instructors. This is probably because the pitch of a woman's or child's voice is far easier for a cockatiel to imitate than the voice of a man or a post-pubescent boy.

Distractions

It is a widely accepted theory that covering a bird's cage with a cloth or newspaper, so that it cannot see the teacher, helps a bird to learn words more quickly. I don't believe this to be the case (again, based on my own personal experience). I am convinced that a bird likes to hear and see its trainer. If you feel your bird learns better when it cannot see you, however, then by all means screen off the cage. Covering both the rear and sides of the cage has the obvious advantage that the bird will not be distracted by anything else going on in the vicinity. Thus, the bird gives you its undivided attention.

Holding Your Bird's Attention

At each training session, you should demand your cockatiel's

attention and set the stage so that you will achieve the best results. Bells, mirrors, and other distracting toys should be put aside while you are training the bird. And never try to train two birds at the same time. Even if they are in different cages, two birds in the same room would rather imitate each other than listen to a human trainer.

Offensive Language

Many keepers of talking birds, for some reason or other, like to teach them obscene or offensive words. Such a practice is very childish and in very bad taste. These trainers should take into consideration the fact that the bird may embarrass them or their families by using such profanity at an inappropriate time or place. It is by no means difficult to teach objectionable language to a bird. The words are often short and have an easily repeated combination of syllables. However, this is a poor excuse for teaching birds things they do not understand and that may offend some people, and adversely affect children.

A Short Training Method

Many people who have trained cockatiels (and other parrots) to speak have come to the conclusion that the process takes much less time than they originally anticipated. By comparison, children often take two or more years to learn to formulate understandable or sensible speech. The prime requirement for quickly teaching your cockatiel to repeat words and phrases is that you have the necessary patience and love for the task before you. For instance, a bird that appears uninterested or is a "difficult" pupil should never be punished but should be treated with love and affection.

The word or short phrase to be taught should be uttered clearly in the same pitch and at the same speed at intervals over a period of about 15 minutes, after which a five-minute break may be taken before proceeding with the same lesson. Other words or expressions should not be used during the lesson. During the break, the lesson should begin to sink in, so make sure there are no other distractions. Do not speak to anyone in the range of the bird's hearing, do not play the radio or TV. Then, after the break, start again and use only the same words or expressions.

After three or four sessions in the morning, the bird can be left to mull over what it has heard until the evening, when you repeat the lessons two or three more times. Do not praise the bird until it has mastered a particular word or expression faultlessly. Apart from the specific speech lessons, it will help if you use an appropriate word or expression each time you enter the room in which the bird is kept. Your "good morning" greeting can be considered as part of the training material, and so can your "good night" as you turn off the light to retire.

If this method of instruction does not seem to work after a reasonable period (three or four days would seem adequate), you will have to try another method. The bird might do better in a half-darkened room, twice a day, in short training sessions of about 30 minutes each. The bird should be able to hear but not see you, and eventually you should be rewarded by hearing the bird repeat what you have taught it. Remember, never lose patience or punish the bird in any way. Any such actions will most likely have an effect opposite to your intentions, because the bird will associate the speech lessons with the punishment. With a single impatient gesture or angry word you can turn your sweet and gentle bird into a nervous, aggressive creature, which will then require even more patience to "come back to normal." Only by treating your animals with the greatest love you can muster will they respond with gratifying obedience, devotion, and affection—which is far more important than any tricks that they might or might not succeed in learning.

Using Bird Psychology

Training a bird will be much easier if you know a little about its psychology and apply this knowledge to the lessons. Remember that the association between time and deed (in this case, the spoken word) is very strong in psittacines and other talking birds. For example, if you want your cockatiel to say "good morning" at the right time of day, it would not make sense to teach it this phrase in the evening! Therefore, use "good morning" only in the mornings, "good night" at night, "good-bye" when someone is leaving, and so on. If you want your bird to repeat the name of a particular type of seed or food, then repeat the name when you serve the food. The bird will then associate the word with that particular type of food and say it only when it sees it. It is interesting to note here that cockatiels (and other parrots), can be taught to use the names of family members correctly!

Many trainers have been very successful with simultaneous taming and speech training. A common method used to do this is as follows: After allowing the new arrival adequate water and food on its first day, remove all food and water dishes from the cage that same evening. Early on the morning of the next day, feed the new bird by hand and give it water, all the while repeating the words you want it to learn. After a while, the cockatiel will associate the words you are teaching it with the fact that it is about to get a good meal, and it will soon learn to repeat your words. When new words are to be taught, the same method can be used, until the bird has "learned to learn." Thereafter it should be a simple matter to teach the bird in the first manner described previously, since the trainer, not the food, will have become the motivation for learning. Thereafter, your presence alone should be enough to incite your feathered friend into performing

its entire repertoire. By rewarding the bird with a little of its favorite food after every performance you will, of course, ensure that it does not lose interest in making appropriate responses to your cues.

Some birds have a habit of refusing to talk every time you come near their cages. A bird may use the repertoire it has been taught to "lure" you to its cage, associating its use of the words with the companionship and affection it craves. Once you arrive at the cage, the bird will consider that its ploy has worked and, thus, feel no further need to talk. If you turn to go away, the bird will begin to talk again, often with a torrent of words and expressions designed to persuade you to stay.

The first few words are the hardest to teach the bird to repeat. Thereafter, however, it will develop an increasing aptitude for learning new words, phrases, and even sentences. You will have to give your cockatiel as much attention as you can, putting continuous effort into teaching it. Without effort, you will not be successful. However, as your friendship with your bird becomes closer, your attention and effort will no longer seem a chore—if they had ever been in the first place—and you will look forward with pleasure to every contact you can have with your little feathered friend.

Tape Recorders and Video Tapes

There are various records, CDs, and video tapes available that give

There are various hospital/nursery units commercially available. They should have thermostat-controlled humidity and temperature levels and circulating air. (Courtesy: Victoria Joseph, DVM)

instructions on training parrots, parakeets, and mynah birds. If you want to have rapid success in teaching your cockatiel to speak, you may find such products useful, especially if you do not have a great deal of time for personal training yourself.

A very good CD is the *Parnami,* especially designed to apply modern technology to the speech training of birds (for information call 215-333-0417 or write to: The Parnami Company, 2147 Magee Avenue, Box A, Philadelphia, PA 19149). Other training and talking CDs of excellent quality are those made by Wordy Birdy Products, 6305 N. O'Connor Blvd., Ste. 119, Irving, TX 75039 (1-800-605-8255). My video tape *The Cockatiel* (ASPC Inc.), is also available in most pet shops. Alterna-

tively, if you have a tape recorder, you can simply record the various words and phrases to be learned, and from then on all you need to do is play the recording as many times as you like until the bird can repeat the words faultlessly. Another advantage of this method is that you can leave the bird on its own while the tape is playing, and it will learn in your absence. If your own voice is on the recording, then of course the bird will think you are present, as it will recognize your own individual intonations. If you do make your tape, be sure to use a tape loop of about six minutes and include plenty of pauses or rest periods so the bird gets a break as the tape will go on forever until you come home to shut it off.

The repetitive talent of a cockatiel (or other mimicking bird species) is not limited to words and phrases. Sooner or later you will notice that your bird is repeating such sounds as, for example, the whistling of another bird, not necessarily its own species. I have known Amazon parrots that would faultlessly mimic the squeaking of a wheelbarrow, the creaking of badly oiled door hinges, and even grandfather's smoker's cough! Any sound that can be imitated will soon attract a bird's attention if the sound is repeated often enough. You may take that, perhaps, as a friendly warning!

Radio and Television

Cockatiels can learn to repeat 40 or more words. They can even speak short sentences at the appropriate moment. However, most parrot-like birds have difficulty in living with a playing radio, television, CD player, or phonograph. In such an environment they will disregard all they have learned and will react by screaming as loudly as they can. If you have more than one bird, the situation becomes even worse: your pets will compete with each other to see who has the loudest scream!

Keep a detailed record of all your birds, and leave a copy at your veterinarian's office. Remember, you and I are able to describe our symptoms to the physician, but the avian veterinarian relies entirely upon his or her powers of observation and those of the bird's owner. (Courtesy: Jeanne Smith, DVM)

Budgies also like to do this. In my home a couple of budgies often try to scream louder than my daughter's piano playing. In contrast, many birds show a certain appreciation for soft, melodious music, and I have seen parrots, budgerigars, and cockatiels swaying their heads as if to keep time with the melody.

Chapter Five

If Your Cockatiel Gets Sick

Although cockatiels are very hardy birds, they will quickly become sick if care and nutrition are lacking in any way. Therefore, you must pay a great deal of attention to ensuring that your birds get the best in housing, feeding, and every other aspect of their care. If you take the time and the trouble to get things right, you have the best chance of avoiding disasters.

The duration of a bird's sickness is often quite short, so if the symptoms of a disease are not quickly noticed, the chances of treating it and nursing the bird back to good health may be lost. Thus, it is important that you familiarize yourself with your birds, learning their attitudes to other birds and what constitutes their normal behavior.

For example, if a bird suddenly starts sitting in spots that it normally avoids, this may be taken as an indication that all is not well. If a bird starts making a bigger mess than usual with its food, this may be a sign that something is wrong. Often, a bird that is sick will sit moping in a corner with its feathers puffed out and with a dull, lifeless look in its eyes. When a healthy bird is resting, it generally sits on just one foot. If your bird sits on both feet, with its eyes partially closed, then it is probably not in good health.

The First Steps

Often there may be only very small indications that a cockatiel is not entirely healthy. Nevertheless, don't hesitate to take appropriate action; it is better to "nip the problem in the bud" than leave it festering. If your diagnosis was incorrect, you have lost nothing other than a little time. Being overconcerned is far better than being nonchalant.

When you notice that one of your cockatiels may be sick, the first step is to isolate it from the other birds in the collection. It is always possible that the bird has contracted a contagious disease that presents a potential danger to all of the birds. One would be well-advised to disinfect the entire bird area, including cages and/or aviaries, food and water containers, perches, toys, and accessories, as soon as a bird has been diagnosed as diseased. The addition of a tonic or multivitamin preparation to the bird's favorite food (or drink) is also a must, but be sure to follow the manufacturer's directions.

The patient should be placed in a separate, small cage, preferably a "hospital cage," the back and sides of which are enclosed and only the front exposed. The cage should preferably have a wire bottom so that the bird's droppings can fall through, thus eliminating the possibility of the bird's soiling itself or even reinfecting itself with its own feces. If necessary, the front can be covered with a cloth to keep in the warmth and maintain a constant temperature. An infrared lamp can be placed 12 to 20 inches (30–50 cm) above the cage. By holding your hand in the line of heat, you can determine if it is too hot for your sick bird. The temperature should be maintained at a constant 85 to 90°F (29–32°C). This can be adjusted by having a thermometer in the cage and raising or lowering the lamp until the desired constant temperature is achieved. As soon as the bird has recovered, the temperature can be gradually reduced back to room temperature by moving the lamp a few inches further away at two-hour intervals and eventually switching it off. Of course, you must ensure that your bird does not catch cold on top of its other problems, so you must avoid drafty situations at all costs.

Difficult-to-diagnose internal diseases also generally pose problems in treatment. Therefore it is advisable to consult an avian veterinarian, who will very likely prescribe an antibiotic that can be dissolved in the bird's drinking water. If the patient should die after all your efforts, it is a good idea to ask your veterinarian where you can have an autopsy performed on the corpse so that, in case of severely contagious diseases, timely prophylactic measures may be taken.

Hospital Cages

There are so-called "hospital cages" available on the market, but with a little skill it is quite possible to make one's own. The best way is to make a glass-fronted box cage 28 inches high, 16 inches wide, and 20 inches deep (70 × 40 × 50 cm). Install a few 60-watt light bulbs wired so that they can work independently of each other. This will enable you to achieve the correct temperature whatever the season.

A thermometer (one that is easy to read) should be affixed to one wall. A sliding tray in the base of the cage can be filled with sand and this should be replaced twice a day, as the droppings of sick birds are likely to be infected with pathogenic organisms. Above the tray install a wire screen through which the bird's droppings can fall. A small door at one end of the cage can be used to give the bird its food and, especially,

What could be ailing this patient? (Courtesy: Jeanne Smith, DVM)

with a nonflammable material to prevent any danger of fire.

Fresh air is very important to a bird confined to such a small, warm space; therefore, drill a few airholes above the little door. Although it is not entirely essential, it is advantageous to have the glass panel or the root attached with hinges so that you have easy access to all parts of the cage. When your patient has recovered, the cage should be thoroughly scrubbed and disinfected inside and out (ensuring, of course, that you have first disconnected the electricity supply!) before putting it away or placing a new patient in it.

water. I say "especially" as the bird will quickly become thirsty in the high temperature and will therefore drink quite a lot. It might be wise to cover the area beneath the bulbs

What to Look For

A careful owner will thoroughly check the interiors of cages, aviaries, perches, and so on at regular intervals for signs of parasites. If these inspections are made every week, being careful not to upset the birds, one may avoid more serious problems later. Cleanliness is absolutely essential! The birds should also be closely inspected, in order to determine whether parasites have gotten into the plumage. Blow some of the feathers aside and look carefully for signs of parasites; you may have to use a magnifying glass. And if the feathers have a brushlike appearance, take action immediately! (See page 109.) Also, if a bird shows signs of losing weight (if its breastbone sticks out, for example), or if a bird becomes over-

Did the bird lose some weight? (Courtesy: Jeanne Smith, DVM)

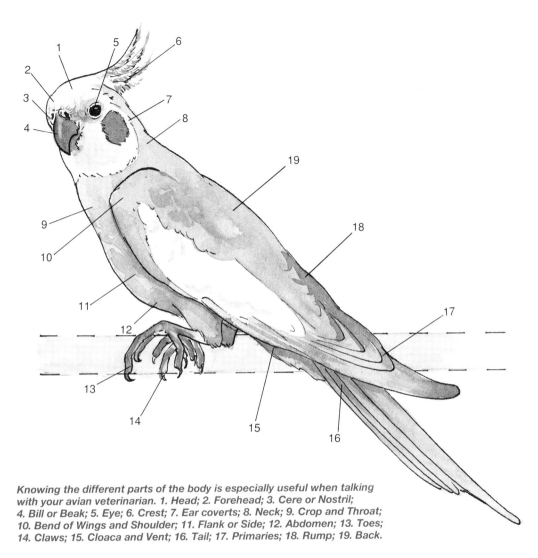

Knowing the different parts of the body is especially useful when talking with your avian veterinarian. 1. Head; 2. Forehead; 3. Cere or Nostril; 4. Bill or Beak; 5. Eye; 6. Crest; 7. Ear coverts; 8. Neck; 9. Crop and Throat; 10. Bend of Wings and Shoulder; 11. Flank or Side; 12. Abdomen; 13. Toes; 14. Claws; 15. Cloaca and Vent; 16. Tail; 17. Primaries; 18. Rump; 19. Back.

weight and has difficulty in moving, you must quickly isolate the bird for individual treatment.

Wet nostrils and a labored, squeaky respiration point to a cold. A gasping beak indicates aspergillosis. Check to see if the eyes have inflamed rims. Carefully palpate legs and wings to see if they are normal. Look under the wings; examine the entire body for wounds or tumors. Check the bird's vent (cloacal opening) regularly for signs of disease. (You can do this visually, without catching the bird.) If the lower part of a hen bird's body is swollen, she is

The internal organs of a cockatiel.
1. Esophagus or Gullet; 2. Crop;
3. Proventriculus; 4. Lungs;
5. Ventriculus or Gizzard;
6. Liver; 7. Spleen; 8. Kidneys;
9. Small intestine; 10. Pancreas;
11. Cloaca; 12. Anus or Vent;
13. Rectum; 14. Large intestine;
15. Gall bladder.

probably suffering from egg binding. If the feathers around the vent are soiled, the bird probably has diarrhea or some other intestinal problem. Of course, a more serious disease may be present. That is why it is important to be able to recognize the major diseases.

Even when a bird has apparently completely recovered from whatever was ailing it, it should not be returned immediately to its normal quarters. After living in warmer quarters as part of the treatment, bringing the bird back to the much cooler temperatures of a cage or aviary would be too much of a shock; the recovered cockatiel would soon become a patient again. As a bird is recovering, allow the temperature in the "sick room" or hospital cage to drop gradually until it reaches the normal temperature of the bird's everyday habitat.

Remember that a bird can starve to death in 24–48 hours; this also applies to sick birds. You must try to get your sick bird to eat and drink, preferably by using a favorite food. Many birds do not die from the effects of the actual disease but from failure to eat!

Preventive Care

Anyone who takes care of sick birds, or comes into contact with them, may become a carrier of an infectious disease. Thus, precautions must be taken. You must wash your hands thoroughly after every treatment or contact. I have often been dismayed to observe how infrequently this simple practice is followed. If just one of your birds had psittacosis or some other contagious disease, and if you merely went from one patient to the next, you would soon have made things a lot worse than they already were. It is only by being meticulous, both with ourselves and our birds, that we birdkeepers can prevent the spread of disease. Even the rubber gloves worn for treatments must be disinfected after each time you have handled a sick bird.

Diseases and Injuries

Aspergillosis

This disease is caused by breathing in spores, particularly of the fungus *Aspergillus fumigatus.* Certain plants, such as those belonging to the genus *Asperula,* can help bring about this fungal infection. Moldy bread ("green" mold), seeds, chaff, musty hay, straw, corncob bedding, and similar items can also cause aspergillosis. The spores produce poisonous toxins that damage tissues in the lungs, nostrils, head cavities, air sacs, etc., causing an accumulation of yellow cheese-like pus that of course interferes with deep and clear breathing. The bird loses all interest in food, with the unfortunate result that it becomes seriously weakened. A bird may even shake its head and stretch out its neck regularly, as if trying to dislodge the blockage. Other symptoms are wheezing, clicking, and respiratory gurgling, increased urination (polyuria), and weight loss. No particularly satisfactory remedy has yet been found for clearing up this problem, and it is best to take your bird to an avian veterinarian.

It is very important to buy fresh seeds, never old or moldy ones. Do not give spilled seed a chance to become moldy; clean the aviary regularly, sweeping up all spilled food. Try to prevent dust and plant spores from blowing into the aviary in spring and fall, particularly if you live near a lumber yard or near any place where hay is stored (you must really beware of wet hay). Whenever a bird has been infected, the entire aviary should be subjected to an intensive inspection followed by a thorough cleaning. Finally, disinfect everything by spraying with a solution including 1 percent copper sulphate before any birds are replaced in the aviary.

Coccidia

Coccidia are microscopic protozoan parasites that occur infrequently in cockatiels. They are spread in the droppings, consumed by the bird, and mature in the intestines. Ordinarily they pose no danger to cockatiels. Birds could be infected for a long time before anyone notices. However, consult an avian veterinarian if you notice a gradually decreased appetite (anorexia), typically coupled with weight loss and loose droppings that may be somewhat bloody. These symptoms could signal a case of coccidiosis. If it is confirmed, sulfa drugs (amprolium and nitrofurazone, for example) may be helpful. It is important to have recently imported birds checked for coccidiosis. Prevention depends on good hygiene and sanitation and a clean, dry floor in the cage or aviary.

Colds

Respiratory difficulties can be brought on by all kinds of problems: drafts, low temperatures, vitamin A and iodine deficiency, stress, and exposure to various bacteria, fungi, and viruses. You will notice the symptoms: A bird will have rapid, audible respiration. Its beak will be open, and its tail will bob up and down. The bird will sneeze and cough, have a nasal discharge, have swollen eyes, and lose its appetite. In most cases, it will sit moping in a corner with its feathers ruffled out.

Such a sick bird requires immediate treatment. Remove it from the cage or aviary, place it in a warm environment, and minimize stress. Remove any discharge from the nostrils by gently dabbing with a cotton ball. Use a vaporizer to spray a fine, warm mist of water into the cage to soothe and moisturize the inflamed lining of the respiratory tract. (A standard vaporizer available at the drugstore is fine.) In any case, consult an avian veterinarian. And check to see that housing, location, feeding, and temperature are up to standard.

Diarrhea

A number of factors can be responsible for intestinal upsets in cockatiels. One of these is bad food—poorly selected or in poor condition because of spoilage or even poison. Other possible causes of diarrhea are obesity, respiratory or intestinal infection, excessive heat, or an excess of protein in the diet. In addition, many bacterial and viral infections cause intestinal disturbances along with other symptoms.

Visible symptoms of impaired intestinal function include listlessness, "hunching," and diarrhea. In serious cases, a bird will no longer rest on a perch but will take to the floor, often sitting in a corner with its head under its wing. The bird may drink quite a bit but will have little appetite for food. The droppings are watery.

It is best to refer all cases of intestinal disturbances to an avian veterinarian, but there are some home remedies you can try. Personally, I have had good success with chamomile tea. You may also give the patient boiled rice, oat flakes, and spray millet. You can also provide rice water instead of the usual drinking water, or you can use a commercial preparation called Norit. Dissolve a tablet of Norit in a tablespoon of water and give the patient one or two drops in the beak, using a feeding syringe or a plastic medicine dropper.

As in other illnesses, move the sick bird to a hospital cage, with the temperature raised to about 90°F (32°C). Together with the antibiotics or other medication prescribed by the veterinarian, quiet and warmth will help the patient recover quickly.

Poorly ventilated quarters in warm weather can also be a cause of intestinal disturbances, as can cold, drafty conditions. Extremes in temperature, especially sudden changes, are a threat to the health of your birds. Cold water is a special problem in outdoor aviaries, especially in harsh climates where your drinking dishes may freeze over and the birds will have to do without water for several hours.

Poisoning can also cause intestinal problems. Birds can be poisoned by spoiled food or by poisonous substances. Be especially careful to avoid exposure to DDT and lindane in insecticides and other chemical sprays. If you suspect your cockatiels have been poisoned, place them in a warm environment and furnish fresh green food and drinking water in which you have dissolved a little bicarbonate of soda (approximately 1 gram per full glass of water). Other good purges include fresh milk or a few drops of Kaopectate or Pepto-Bismol (2–3 drops every four hours). Never provide bicarbonate of soda for more than three days running.

A special type of poisoning may occur when birds consume excessive amounts of protein, especially during the breeding season. The same condition can be brought on by an excess of egg food or soft food. Often a breeder simply forgets that egg food should be provided in addition to, not instead of, the usual feed. Affected birds will suddenly show all of the typical symptoms of poisoning: They seem dull and sleepy, they have trouble breathing, and they cease flying. Often they have severe diarrhea, which can lead to a quick death.

On the one hand, diarrhea can be a symptom of a great many avian diseases; on the other hand, you don't have to suspect serious disease problems if the only symptom you notice is the diarrhea. If there are no other indications of a specific serious illness, it can simply be a case of ordinary indigestion.

A watery discharge is not always diarrhea. Cockatiels may be reacting to fear, to being picked up by hand, or even to having taken in too much liquid. Still if you notice diarrhea, the safest response is to consult an avian veterinarian.

Discolored and Deformed Feathers

A shortage of vitamin A and the amino acid (protein) lysine is often the cause of feather development problems (cockatiels that are fed exclusively on sunflower seeds always end up with very bad plumage). With correct nutrition, the birds will develop healthy, well-formed, colorful, sleek plumage after their first molt. If this is not the case, and the feathers grow out of the shafts in a twisted, frayed condition, it is possible that the bird is suffering Psittacine Beak and Feather Disease, a viral disease that, at the present time, affects mainly parrot-like birds. Birds infected with the polyoma virus also may grow malformed feathers. In both cases, the birds must be immediately isolated and an avian veterinarian must be consulted.

E. coli Infections

Infections with *Escherichia coli,* enteric (gram-negative) bacteria, generally known as *E. coli,* can pose serious problems for cockatiels. *E. coli*'s principal victims are humans, but birds are not immune. Don't let anyone tell you that *E. coli* are normal residents of the bird's intestines. They are not. And if they spread to the lungs, liver, and heart, they can cause a speedy death.

The best preventive is good hygiene. Wash your hands before you move birds, prepare feed, inspect nests, or carry out any other activities with your birds. Prevent fecal contamination and avoid spoiled food, dirty water, dirty perches, dirty nest boxes, dirty floors in cages and aviaries, and other sources of contamination.

Treatment consists of 3–4 drops of Kaopectate or Pepto-Bismol every four hours, administered with a plastic medicine dropper. This will soothe and coat the inflamed digestive tract. Seek veterinary assistance if rapid improvement is not observed within 24 hours; the vet may prescribe use of the many antibiotics that can provide relief.

Egg Binding

Cockatiels that are properly housed and fed will rarely be troubled with egg binding—a problem that causes the affected bird to be unable to lay an egg that is ready to come out. The affected female looks sick, sits hunched up, usually on the floor (seldom in the nest box), moves little, and in most cases is easy to catch by hand. If you feel her abdomen, you will quickly notice the trouble—the stuck egg.

In the normal course of events, an egg spends no more than 24 hours in the wide section of the ovary leading to the cloaca and in the cloaca itself. At the proper time, the muscles in the lowest part of the ovary push it into the cloaca and then, in a short time, entirely out of the body.

The muscles involved can fail to function properly as a result of a cold, stress (such as chilling), over-breeding, poor muscle tone (old age or being out of condition), or a deficiency of calcium and/or certain vitamins. The affected bird will try valiantly to lay the egg, but in vain.

Another form of egg binding can result from shell-less or thin-shelled eggs ("wind" eggs). This condition can be caused by some malfunction in the deposit of calcium on the egg or by a calcium shortage in the hen's body. The weak or absent shell tends to cause the egg to get stuck because the muscles in the ovary and cloaca can't get a good grip on the soft mass.

Egg binding is entirely preventable under normal circumstances. Clearly, planning is necessary to prevent any shortage of vitamins or minerals. Be sure that while the bird is breeding it has a balanced diet, including an adequate supply of green food and sprouted seed. To prevent wind eggs, ensure that your birds have enough calcium, especially calcium phosphate. Commercial bird grit contains the key minerals, including calcium, so you really don't have to do more than ensure that there is always plenty of grit in the cage or aviary. Cuttlebone should also be available at all times, and during the breeding season, a little bread and milk with grated cheese will be appreciated.

A further caution to reduce the possibility of egg binding is not to start breeding your birds too early in the season. The temperature and humidity are probably not ideal so early. In the colder states it is advisable not to start breeding until the end of March or early to mid-April. Also, never breed females that are too young. Immature birds are extremely likely candidates for egg binding.

Fortunately, egg binding is entirely curable, provided you act fast enough. First, use a plastic dropper to put a few drops of warm mineral oil in the cloaca, so that the egg can move along more smoothly. Second, transfer the hen to a hospital cage and raise the temperature to about 90°F (32°C) with an infrared lamp. Warmth should help your patient to recover. Even better, consult an avian veterinarian as soon as you notice any sign of egg binding. By injecting the bird with calcium and other medicines, the vet may be able to stimulate the contractions of the oviduct. Sometimes the vet may even recommend surgical removal of the egg.

Note: Do not use an "artificially laid" egg for brooding.

Egg Pecking

Cockatiels occasionally peck at eggs lying in the nest. Take immediate action and remove the offending bird from the cage or aviary. There is no known cause for egg pecking, but I am sure that the chances of its occurring are very small if you provide proper feeding, housing, nurturing, and recreation.

Eye Disease

Cockatiels are subject to several types of eye infections. In most cases, the problem results from complications of colds and resulting side infections caused by bacteria and viruses. Other possible causes are a deficiency in vitamin A or the use of aerosol sprays or dusty seed that irritates the eye. A bird will generally close the affected eyes, which will be teary and have inflamed edges (blepharitis).

Bacterial infections often start as a result of dirty perches. The bird can easily pick up an infection by wiping its beak along a dirty perch. Another factor in the spread of eye infections is the shipment of large consignments of birds in a small, crowded box—so look for trouble in recently imported birds. This type of infection causes the edges of generally just one eye to be heavily inflamed.

Take action immediately when your cock-atiel's eyes have inflamed rims. Using a soft cotton swab, carefully apply an antibiotic ointment.

Place the bird in a warm environment, preferably in a hospital cage. Rinse the eyes with 5 percent boric acid, or apply an antibiotic ophthalmic ointment two or three times a day (ophthalmic Neosporin or Neopolycin are good commercial products). A few days of treatment are usually sufficient to assure a speedy recovery. It can't hurt to consult an avian veterinarian about the problem.

Knemidokoptes mites (see Scaly Face, page 115) can also indirectly irritate eyelids and eyes when the typical scabs occur in the eye region. Treat the scabs and the edges of the eye with an ophthalmic penicillin ointment.

A deficiency of vitamin A in the diet can lead to wartlike little bumps on the eyelids. Improvement of the diet will help, but in any case, the sick bird should be isolated as these little warts can also be a symptom of psittacine pox, a contagious disease that must be treated by an avian veterinarian.

Serious cases of eye infection can lead to complete blindness in one or both eyes. This result is usually preceded by heavy tearing, after which the afflicted eye's pupil turns milky white. Birds that become partially or totally blind can be kept alive in a small cage. In the beginning, place food and water on the floor of the cage, preferably in a shallow earthenware dish. Although it takes a while, the blind bird eventually adjusts.

Feather Cysts

Another condition that sometimes occurs in cockatiels is feather cysts.

These growths, which are not to be confused with tumors, are caused by the growth of a feather shaft inside the feather follicle. The feather curls up under the skin and does not break through. The more the feather grows under the skin, the greater the size of the cyst. If opened up, the cyst will be found to contain a cheeselike substance. A cyst that remains untreated will eventually break open, so there is a possibility of secondary infection. In some cases, the bird itself will peck the cyst open. The resultant exudate hardens on contact with the air and forms a scab, which continues to grow with the feather. Eventually it will drop off.

Birds with several feather cysts should have them and the abnormal feathers removed surgically by an avian veterinarian. Any bleeding that occurs can be stopped by using styptic wadding or even by fine cauterization. With large wounds, especially those caused by the removal of whole, unbroken cysts, it may be necessary to suture the edges of the wound together. Such operations are generally followed by a systemic course of antibiotic treatment. Cysts on the back or on the tail are best removed wholly; this operation can be performed under local anesthesia, though this is not always necessary.

Feather Plucking or Picking

Feather plucking frequently occurs toward the end of a normal or abnormal molt. It is not difficult to understand that these dermatological processes cause itching, then

An Elizabethan collar is used for really persistent feather-pluckers. The bird usually gets used to the device within a few days.

scratching, then feather plucking. Thereafter, a bird may continue plucking feathers simply to relieve boredom. Admittedly, the latter explanation has no sound scientific basis, but so far there appears to be no other reason for the phenomenon. It remains a fact that cockatiels with "nothing else to do" sometimes become habitual feather pluckers and within a few weeks can strip themselves almost naked! Most parrot-like birds can develop the habit, but especially cockatiels and cockatoos.

Feather plucking usually begins with the bird plucking out a few old feathers that must be removed (at least the bird thinks so!). Then the bird advances to new, perhaps undeveloped feathers. This produces itching and, possibly, pleasurable or stimulating sensations, and then there is no end! Many feathers may be gnawed off at the base, leaving just stumps. These stumps inhibit the growth of new feathers and must be removed, especially from the wings. To do this, hold the wing firmly with one hand and with a pair of forceps pull the feather stump out at right angles. Have some wadding available to stop bleeding. In some cases, it may be necessary to use a styptic (blood coagulating) preparation to stop the bleeding. Sometimes a bird can bleed seriously after gnawing at the base of a new feather. Wing and tail feathers are responsible for the worst cases of bleeding. A suffering bird can quickly weaken from loss of blood. If you do not take immediate action, there is a danger that the bird will die from blood loss.

It is an interesting fact to note that most feather-plucking cockatiels—at least in the United States—are also infected with giardiasis, an intestinal protozoan parasite that causes pruritis (severe itching of the undamaged skin), which leads to feather plucking. European cockatiels seem to rarely suffer from pruritis.

The first recourse to discourage feather plucking is to give the birds something to keep them occupied. Hang several thick pieces of sisal string or rope in the aviary; give them twigs from fruit trees, from willow and privet. The birds will happily occupy themselves playing with and nibbling these goodies. Improve the diet, especially by providing additional minerals, proteins, vitamins,

and amino acids. Willow twigs contain lignine, an amino acid that is effective in curing feather pluckers.

Other avenues of approach are to make sure that the temperature is not too low and the humidity not too high; that there is good light and ventilation in the birds' accommodation; that the birds have adequate bathing facilities (a weak spray from a hose, especially on warm days, is strongly recommended); and that the accommodation is not so cluttered with plants, utensils, and other items that the birds do not have freedom of movement. Persistent feather pluckers must have an Elizabethan collar, which can be made from stout cardboard, affixed around the neck to prevent their reaching their plumage with their beaks but still allowing them to feed and drink. After a few weeks with a collar and improved diet and accommodations, the bird is likely to have lost its desire to pluck its feathers. Sometimes feather plucking is caused by the birds being hypersexed and frustrated—a hormonal situation. If all other solutions fail, your veterinarian may recommend the judicious use of progesterone.

Feather plucking can lead to cannibalism. It is therefore most important to remove all damaged feathers from the bird; new feathers will replace them in six to eight weeks. If the damaged feathers are left on the bird, it will gnaw away at them until sooner or later it will damage its skin, causing serious bleeding and opening the way to the possibility of secondary infection. Lovebirds, grass parakeets, and rosellas as well as cockatiels may also develop the habit of plucking their young to baldness. It is not unusual in such cases to see that the young leaving the nest are totally bald on the neck, head, and part of the back. In serious cases, the flight and tail feathers may also be plucked out, with possible damage to the feather follicles. Replacement feathers will then grow in an abnormally twisted manner.

There are commercially available sprays that have a nasty taste and are said to prevent the adults from plucking their young. This claim seems doubtful when one considers that a bird's sense of taste is poorly developed. Some adults are really persistent in plucking the feathers of their young. All that can be done in such cases is to remove the young and place them in the care of reliable parents. If no foster parents are available, the youngsters can be separated from their parents by a cage with a mesh of sufficient gauge for the parents to feed the young through it.

Fractures

Fractures of the leg or wing can be avoided by handling birds gently and protecting them from barking dogs and prowling cats. If an accident should happen, consult an avian veterinarian, especially if you are a beginner to birdkeeping.

If your veterinarian is not available, and you feel capable of treating a broken leg yourself, line up the severed sections and splint the fracture on either side of the leg with a couple of thin sticks (wooden matches or pieces of bamboo skewer are ideal). Keep the splints in place by winding gauze around the leg and binding it with surgical tape. Wind the gauze tightly; the idea is to restrict movement at the point of fracture as much as possible.

Any bandage allows some movement. To avoid this as much as possible, I prefer an alternative method. I wrap the fractured leg in small strips of gauze that have been treated with a thin preparation of plaster of Paris. First, wrap the leg twice, line it up properly, and hold it in place until the plaster sets. Then wrap another couple of strips around the fracture. Since it is more difficult to deal with a fracture occurring close to the bird's body, it may be especially useful to use the gauze-plus-plaster method in these cases. Better yet, these tricky fractures should be brought to your avian veterinarian for treatment.

Sometimes it is easy to mistake a torn muscle for a broken leg. This condition can occur when a bird makes desperate movements to free itself after being caught in wire mesh (often the result of overgrown nails). Torn muscles do not heal easily. You can try to immobilize the affected leg with a bandage, keeping it stable while nature takes its course.

A bird with a leg injury should be kept in a hospital cage without perches until the healing process is complete. Cover the cage bottom with peat moss. Darken the cage partially and place it in a quiet location, so that the injured bird will move as little as possible. Be sure that the diet contains an adequate amount of vitamins and minerals.

Broken, drooping wings can best be bandaged with gauze. Cut a slit in the gauze, then put the folded wing through the slit. Wrap gauze around the body and secure it to a leg to keep it from sliding off. Make sure the bandage is tight without pinching the bird. Wing fractures also require the placement of the patient in a dark, quiet spot for several weeks. Use a cage that is without perches and that is low enough to prevent the bird from flying. Although most birds will get used to the treated leg or wing, some patients will have to wear an Elizabethan collar to keep them from pecking at the injury.

Again, setting a broken wing is a difficult task, and it is better to entrust it to a veterinarian. The treatment I have suggested is likely to keep the wing in its proper position, but the bird may not be able to fly afterward.

French Molt or BFD*

French molt is known by most bird fanciers, although it is fortunately uncommon in lovebirds and cockatiels. It normally starts in young birds while they are still in the nest. Many theories as to the cause of French

*Budgerigar Fledgling Disease

molt have been suggested, but there is now evidence that an avian polyoma virus is the culprit. In most cases of French molt, a bird that is about to leave the nest and fledge will suddenly shed or break its newly acquired tail and flight feathers. Generally, it is the primary flight feathers and the tail feathers that are affected, but in serious cases, the secondary feathers are also included. Totally featherless birds are also not unknown! It is a pathetic sight to see these naked or half-naked birds running about. In contrast, some cases of French molt are so mild as to be almost or completely undetectable; some birds just lose a few tail feathers and are still able to fly. It is interesting to note that in French molt the feathers are often lost symmetrically. A daily inspection of the patients will show that the inner primaries are usually the first affected. Only growing feathers are lost; fully grown ones are not affected.

What can be done about French molt? The answer is disappointing—nothing or very little. You may breed cockatiels for many years without seeing a sign of French molt, and then suddenly, it may appear among your birds without any apparent cause. It is interesting to note that some pairs of birds in the same aviary produced perfectly healthy youngsters, although they had exactly the same feeding, housing, and care as the affected birds. The only remedy is to stop the breeding, separate the birds, and allow them to rest for at least six months.

Frostbite

Cold winter days (and nights) pose the possibility of frozen toes. Frostbite may occur when the cockatiels hang onto the wire mesh for too long, something they tend to do if they are startled. Perches that are too thin may also cause problems because the birds' toes are partially bare and thus not protected by feathers. Obviously you need to replace the perches in such cases. If you use sleeping boxes, cover the bottom with an insulating layer of peat moss.

In cases of frostbite, there is not much you can do other than to consult a veterinarian, who may prescribe a salve. The frozen part becomes dark and stiff, dries out and drops off without any apparent harm to the bird. At the first sign of infection, treat the wound immediately with noncaustic iodine.

Goiter

Goiter, which is an abnormal enlargement of the thyroid gland, used to be particularly common among captive cockatiels, Australian grass parakeets (rosellas, Bourke's, and others), lovebirds, and budgerigars. Fortunately, the condition is no longer a frequent occurrence as commercial cage sand is usually treated with iodine. The problem may still occur, however, in areas where drinking water is deficient in iodine.

You can usually recognize goiter by external swelling of a bird's neck. The growth, pressing against crop and windpipe, is internal, and any exertion such as flying and running will make the bird breathless very quickly. Breathing heavily, it will drop to the ground, often with widespread wings and pendulous crop and neck. It may also make a high-pitched squeak or wheezing sound with each breath. To help itself breathe more easily, the bird will often rest its beak against the bars of the cage or on a parallel perch or tree branch.

The condition will worsen if you fail to act immediately. The bird may start to walk in circles—an indication of cerebral infection. Sudden death might then follow, caused by asphyxiation, heart failure, or weakness due to insufficient intake of food. In the case of a serious thyroid disorder, give the bird iodine glycerine. The proper mixture for cockatiels is one part tincture of iodine to five parts glycerine. As an alternative, a mixture of nine parts paraffin oil to one part iodine glycerine, administered with a plastic dropper in a corner of the beak intermittently over a period of three days, usually works wonders. A Lugol's solution added to the drinking water also works well. If the condition persists, see your avian veterinarian.

Mites

Feather mites are divided into nondisease mites, which live on the skin as well as on the feathers, and very small mites, which can burrow into the shaft and follicle.

The first, *Syringophilus bipectioratus,* may be found in wild birds, cockatiels, canaries, and pigeons. It

Checking wings and other "outer parts" of the bird's body.

feeds on feather and skin debris and can cause irritation that leads to feather plucking. The second, *Dermoglyphus elongatus,* burrows into the feather structure.

There is but one sure therapy for feather mites. Keep your aviary as clean as possible. Let the birds bathe as much as they want, and keep wild birds away by whatever means are available. These precautions will help control the red bird-mite *Dermanyssus gallinae.* This so-called surface-dwelling mite shelters during the day in cracks and crevices, in perches and nest boxes, and then emerges at night to torment the birds by feeding on their blood. A single mite does not take a lot of blood, but in numbers these pests can cause untold damage,

weakening your birds and spreading disease. Nesting birds can be constantly and severely tormented by these bloodsucking mites. It is therefore important that at each cleaning session you examine all parts of your cages, aviaries, utensils, etc., for signs of mites. A magnifying glass will certainly help you. Cover a cage with a white cloth at night and check the following day to see if there are any tiny red spots on the cloth. If there are, the cloth must be burned or soaked in petroleum and then washed in detergent before being used again. And you must clean and spray your bird areas.

The red bird-mite can live for weeks or even months without a blood meal. At such times the mites are difficult to detect since they are translucent until they have the chance to feed on blood again. In temperatures of 68°F (20°C), the mites can reproduce every five days. They can survive in outdoor aviaries even in times of severe frost. Red mites (and other mite species) can be introduced to your aviary at any time by wild birds such as sparrows, starlings, and pigeons sitting on the aviary roof and preening their plumage. Or they can be introduced with new stock, especially birds from large stock aviaries.

Many insecticides are effective against red mites. Most of them contain pyrethrin, made from the pyrethrum flower, a kind of chrysanthemum. Thus, pyrethrin is a natural substance, which is harmless to birds. Pyrethrin is also effective against ticks, lice, fleas, and mites. Apply it to all parts of cages, aviaries, utensils, etc. While treating your birds, pay special attention to the neck, to the area around the vent, and under the wings. Do not put birds back into their old quarters until everything there is completely dry. Repeat the treatment after several days to be sure that you eliminate any insect eggs.

Molt

Molt is not a disease condition. The feathers of cockatiels are subject to a great deal of wear and tear. The effects of weather and wind (temperature, humidity, photoperiod), preening, nesting, the young creeping between them for warmth, and other activities all take their toll on a cockatiel's feathers. That is why they change their plumage once a year. In fact, parrot-like birds molt during the whole year, with the high point coming after the breeding season when the young have become independent. One can conclude from this that the functions of the sex organ (testicles, ovaries, etc.) are closely related to the molt. In addition, a normal, problem-free molt is dependent on the season, the temperature, the humidity, and the bird's diet. One should note that the molt is more intense after a warm spring and good beginning to the summer than it is during cold and wet months. In some cases, a bird is so eager to molt that it will continually fluff out and shake its feathers, even going so far as to

Healthy birds will preen themselves several times a day. During molt, however, they also will remove little feathers.

pluck them out with its beak, clearly deriving some relief from so doing. Normally, however, this is usually a restful time for birds, when they will avoid unnecessary activity. Research has shown that a bird's body temperature may sink. During this period, the birds require a diet rich in protein (feathers consist of 88 percent protein). They are also susceptible to bone fractures, owing to the resorption of calcium from the bone tissue. As new feathers are formed from protein, there is the possibility that a bird receiving insufficient rations will use them to supplement its diet!

Occasionally, a bird may lose too many feathers at once and have difficulty in replacing them. Such a molt is called an abnormal molt. A bird that loses feathers in the wrong season is also suffering from abnormal molt. In most cases, these abnormal molts are caused by extreme environmental factors such as unusually high or low temperatures, sudden weather changes, shock, disease, or fear. One of the most common causes of abnormal molt is a malfunction of the thyroid gland. See your veterinarian, who will determine whether a dietary supplement is needed.

Another kind of molt is the so-called shock molt, in which the bird suddenly starts losing feathers outside the normal molting time. Such shedding may occur if the bird is subjected to shock or fear; therefore, it is best to treat your birds carefully and gently, especially those that have just been acquired and are still finding their way around.

Young birds should also be left in peace so that they gradually but surely get accustomed to their keeper and their surroundings. It is therefore essential not to disturb the birds at night. Cats, owls, weasels, mice, rats, and the like must be kept away from the aviary so that they do not frighten the birds and possibly cause a shock molt. I have frequently seen birds contract shock molt after being removed at night to be treated for a totally different disease! With shock molt, the bird usually loses tail feathers and smaller body feathers but, remarkably, seldom wing feathers. The shedding of tail feathers can be compared with autotomy (or tail shedding) in many lizard species. A predator ends up with a mouthful of tail feathers as the bird makes its escape.

Sometimes it is possible for a cockatiel to have a permanent molt. This is usually caused by a shortage of various amino acids in the bird's diet. In such cases, the normal molt may also be incomplete. Correcting the diet will generally solve the problem. Plant and animal proteins are necessary, and a good vitamin/mineral supplement should be offered at frequent and regular intervals. The birds must be comfortably housed and protected from cold, wind, and wide swings in temperature. In the colder months, supplementary heating (in the form of ceramic lamps, for example) can be provided. Use of a Vita-Lite has a beneficial effect on the health and vitality of the birds. Vita-Lite is a fluorescent lamp that produces the whole color spectrum of natural sunlight and approximately a similar number of microwatts of ultraviolet per lumen. In addition, Vita-Lite offers the biological advantages of natural sunlight, something that other artificial lights do not have. A light with the whole color spectrum (especially the ultraviolet part) can have significant influence on the bird's biological functions, including the production of vitamins in the body and the fixing of calcium in the bone tissues. It is a scientific fact that the quality of light plays an important part in satisfactory biological functions. I therefore have no hesitation in recommending

Vita-Lite as a necessary acquisition for bird fanciers who keep their pets indoors.

Obesity

Birds that lack exercise because of their cage being too small, or because they do not have enough toys to keep them occupied, may become too fat. Birds that do not receive proper nutrition are also likely to fall victim to obesity.

The process of becoming too fat is very slow. Owners must be alert and watch carefully for the first signs of obesity. When a bird can hardly sit on its perch, things have already gone too far. The bird might sit on the cage bottom, lethargic and panting heavily. The contours of its body become blurred, heavy, and cylindrical, and the skin appears yellowish when the feathers on the breast or abdomen are blown aside. This is the fat shining through the skin.

Birds suffering from obesity live much shorter lives than those that have plenty of exercise and lively interests. The obese bird has difficulty molting and generally just sits, looking thoroughly bored.

You must keep your birds from getting fat, or, if some are already overweight, you must take corrective action. The first thing to do is to give the birds plenty of exercise. Caged cockatiels must be released daily in a secure area and allowed to fly freely for at least an hour. Birds kept in a cage or (small) aviary must have even more exercise. Consider housing them in larger cages or placing perches farther apart. Hang some strong sisal ropes in the cage, along with a few branches of spray millet or weed seeds. Cockatiels love to play with these.

The second anti-obesity action to take is to improve your birds' nutrition (strictly by the book, if necessary), providing lots of well-washed greens or fruit free of chemicals. Do not provide food with a high protein or fat content. And do not work from the assumption, "My bird is fat, so if I don't feed it for a few days it will be all right again." The bird must be fed, but with the right kind of food. It will perish, however fat it might be, if it receives no nourishment.

Poisoning

See Diarrhea, page 100.

Preen Gland, Infections of

Occasionally, the preen gland can become infected. An abscess may form if the orifice becomes blocked. In such cases, a marked swelling on the tail stump will become apparent, and the bird will be in obvious pain. A suffering bird will peck and scratch at the offending spot on its tail and may even pluck out feathers adjacent to the gland. After a time, the abscess may burst, leaving signs of blood on perches and other areas the bird inhabits. The conscientious cockatiel keeper must not let the problem get to this stage. A chronic infection usually arises from overproduction of the preening secretion, so we can relieve the symptoms to some extent by gently squeezing out the gland at frequent intervals. If gentle squeezing does not help, it will be necessary to consult an avian veterinarian, who will cut open the abscess with a scalpel and then squeeze out the contents. An application of antibiotics and something to stop the bleeding will be necessary.

With these same symptoms, it is also possible that there is a tumor on the preen gland. These are usually benign, but in such cases the veterinarian must operate, being careful that not too much blood is lost.

Psittacosis

Psittacosis is a disease of parrots and parakeets that is called ornithosis in other bird species. It occurs only rarely in cockatiels.

This serious disease is caused by an obligate intracellular parasite, *Chlamydia psittaci,* distinguished from all other microorganisms by its unique growth cycle. Psittacosis occurs especially in dirty breeding operations and can be brought in by imported birds, especially smuggled birds. Be suspicious of dirty-looking birds. They may seem healthy, but a careful examination may reveal that they are infected.

Psittacosis can have a variety of symptoms, and therefore it is difficult to diagnose, especially in its early stages. Usually it starts with a heavy cold. Moisture drips from the nostrils, the bird gasps for air, and its breathing is squeaky and hissing. The bird looks worn out and often has diarrhea. Before the disease becomes fatal, there are often symptoms of cramps and lameness.

There is a mild form of psittacosis that can often be completely cured. However, be aware that recovered birds can be infectious for both other birds and humans. Any case of the disease can pose a hazard, which is why you are required to report any suspicion of psittacosis to a veterinarian or the U.S. Public Health Service.

Human beings can contract psittacosis, too. The disease usually starts with cold symptoms and can progress to a lung infection. In earlier times, the disease was dangerous. The advent of antibiotics has removed this danger, provided you get timely diagnosis and treatment. In the mid-1960s, many countries imposed strong restrictions on the importation of hookbills. In general, imported parrots have to be quarantined for 30 days on arrival and are given a preventive treatment with chlortetracycline. Infected birds are treated for 45 days with this drug.

Salmonella

Salmonella causes many fatalities in young cockatiels. The rodlike salmonella bacteria cause diarrhea, painful joints, and nervous disorders. The bacteria are passed in the droppings of infected birds, or via the saliva (by parent birds feeding their young). Salmonella organisms can also enter the eggs.

There are four forms of the disease, which can all occur at the same time. *Intestinal form:* The bacteria enter the wall of the intestine.

Diarrhea is the result, with foul-smelling, soupy, green or brown droppings surrounded by slime and containing undigested food particles. (A green color in the droppings can also indicate a gallbladder infection. Consult a veterinarian immediately!) *Joint form:* A strong intestinal infection can result in the bacteria entering the bloodstream and infecting all parts of the body, including the bone joints. The result is pain and intense swelling. The infected bird attempts to relieve the pain by not using the wings and the feet. *Organ form:* Once the bacteria enter the bloodstream they can infect all internal organs, especially the liver, kidneys, pancreas, heart, and various other glands. The sick bird becomes inactive, mopes in a corner of the cage or aviary, becomes short of breath and nearsighted. *Nervous form:* Salmonella can infect the nerves and spinal column, causing loss of balance and crippling. The awkward turning of the neck, fouling of the cloaca, and cramplike contractions of the toes are typical symptoms.

Cockatiels infected with salmonella get serious intestinal problems in three to four days. The bacteria multiply in the intestinal lining and eventually migrate into the bloodstream. Fatalities occur quickly in young birds, which have no immunity. Older birds, however, incubate the disease over a long period, and if they are not adequately cured, will become carriers capable of infecting other birds via their oviducts and their droppings.

Heavy losses of young birds during the breeding season are a sign of salmonellosis in the stock. A veterinarian should be called immediately to examine blood samples and dead birds.

Scaly Face

Scaly face is caused by burrowing mites *(Knemidokoptes pilae),* which attack the skin area around the eyes and beak and also, in serious cases, the legs and toes. These little arachnoidal parasites burrow into the outer layers of the skin, where they lay their eggs. If untreated, the resulting rough, scaly growths will gradually increase, and severe deformities of the beak can occur. The condition will spread from one bird to another if no preventive action is taken.

Benzyl benzoate, petroleum jelly, or glycerine can be applied to the crusty, honeycomblike scales. Mineral oil can also be used, but be careful to daub it only on the infected area; don't drip any oil on the plumage. (Use a cotton-tipped applicator.) In serious cases, consult an avian veterinarian, who will treat the infection with Eurax Cream or with Ivermectin (Equalan), an injectable medication.

Remove any scaly scabs that fall off as quickly as possible, and burn them if you can. Then avoid further spreading by cleaning the cage, perches, sleeping boxes, and nest boxes. Scaly face is not a dangerous infection, but it is a troublesome one that merits great care to be sure it is completely eradicated. Fortunately, cockatiels seem to be less frequently infected with scaly face than budgerigars, in which the disease is quite common.

Sour Crop

Sour crop is usually the result of a blockage of the crop-exit, due to something the bird has eaten—a small feather, for example. The crop contents start to ferment, releasing carbon dioxide. As a result the crop becomes swollen with gas. The patient vomits a frothy liquid, and its head and beak become stained with mucus. The patient should be held head down, and the crop gently massaged to drive out the gas and some of the accumulated fluid (which is mainly water). Keep the bird warm and offer it water, to which some potassium permanganate has been added.

If you suspect that one of your cockatiels may have sour crop, consult your avian veterinarian as soon as possible.

Worms

Worm infections in birds in outdoor aviaries are hard to avoid. The worms are brought in by wild birds that perch on the aviary and let their droppings fall inside.

Roundworms (Ascaris) start as long, white larvae that grow to adulthood in the intestines of birds that swallow them. The adult worms, in turn, lay eggs that exit from the bird's body in their droppings. Infested birds quickly lose weight, develop poor feathering, and may

suffer from diarrhea or constipation. To confirm a parasite infection, take a stool sample to your avian veterinarian, who is likely to prescribe piperazine or levamisole. The best prevention is first-rate hygiene and sanitation. If the aviary floor is made of concrete, regular hosing down will remove any infected droppings.

Threadworms (Capillaria) start as round, threadlike parasites that attain adulthood in the crop or intestine of the bird. Adult worms lay eggs, which leave the bird's body in the droppings. Signs of infestation include diarrhea and loss of weight. Confirm the problem by having a stool sample analyzed. Again, the veterinarian is likely to prescribe piperazine or levamisole, and prevention depends on excellent hygiene and sanitation. To clean floors use Clorox in a dilution of 6 ounces per gallon of water (a 9 percent solution); this may be corrosive to bare metal.

Basic Medications

Gevral Protein, for appetite loss. Always mix with Mull Soy, which is also a good source of essential vitamins and minerals. Use one part Gevral Protein to three parts Mull Soy. Tube feed 2–3 mL, two or three times daily. Ask your veterinarian for details.

Kaopectate or *Pepto-Bismol,* for loose droppings and regurgitation. Soothes and coats the digestive tract, and helps to form a solid stool. Two or three drops every four hours, administered with a plastic medicine dropper.

Maalox or *Digel,* for crop disorders. Soothes the inflammation and eliminates gas. Dosage: 2 or 3 drops every four hours.

Karo Syrup, for dehydration and as provider of energy. Add 4 drops to 1 quart (1 L) of water. Administer 8–10 drops slowly in the mouth every 20–30 minutes with a plastic medicine dropper.

Monsel solution or *styptic powder,* for bleeding. But don't use styptic powder for areas near the beak.

Milk of Magnesia, for constipation. Do not use milk of magnesia if your bird has kidney problems or heart disease. Consult your veterinarian. Dosage: 3 to 5 drops in the mouth with a plastic dropper, twice daily for two days.

Mineral oil, for constipation, crop impaction, or egg binding. Use 2 drops in the mouth for two days with a plastic dropper. Be very careful when administering the oil, as it can cause pneumonia and vitamin deficiency if it enters the breathing tubes and lungs.

Hydrogen peroxide, 3 percent, activated charcoal (of milk of magnesia), for poisoning. To induce vomiting, to absorb the substance, and to speed its passage through the digestive tract. Ask your avian veterinarian for more details.

Goodwinol; mineral oil; Scalex; Eurax; Vaseline, for scaly face and/or scaly leg.

Betadine; Domeboro solution; A&D ointment; Neosporin; Neopolycin; Mycitracin; Aquasol A, for skin irritations. Domeboro is used on a wet dressing: dissolve 1 teaspoon or tablet in a pint of water. A&D is excellent for small areas. Neosporin, Neopolycin, and Mycitracin contain antibiotics. Aquasol A is a cream and contains vitamin A. All these ointments and creams can be applied to the affected area twice daily.

Lugol's iodine solution, for thyroid enlargement (goiter). Half a teaspoon of Lugol with 1 ounce of water; place 1 drop of this mixture in 1 ounce of drinking water daily for two to three weeks.

Other Health Necessities

Heat source: Infrared lamp (60–100 watt bulb).

Hospital cage: several commercial models are available. Ask your avian veterinarian or pet store manager for advice.

Environmental thermometer: buy one that is easy to read, so that you can accurately monitor the temperature in the hospital cage.

Cage covering: use a cage covering if you do not have a hospital cage. Towels or baby blankets are fine, as are a number of commercial covers. Drape these over an open bird cage.

Adhesive or *masking tape:* use a half-inch roll.

Sterile gauze pads
Cotton-tipped swabs

Needle-nosed pliers and/or *tweezers*

Sharp scissors with rounded ends (baby nail scissors)

Feeding tubes: use 8F or 10F tubes, which many veterinarians carry. Ask your veterinarian to demonstrate the technique of tube feeding.

Syringes or *plastic medicine droppers:* for administering oral medication.

If you want to learn about new developments in the field of avian medicine, contact your veterinarian or:

Association of Avian Veterinarians
P.O. Box 811720
Boca Raton, FL 33481-1720
Tel: (561) 393-8901
(see also page 177).

Chapter Six

Breeding Cockatiels

Introduction

When you move your birds from breeding cage to aviary or vice versa, ask one of your colleagues from the bird society to do it for you! Yes, you have read correctly; let the work be done by a friend and don't do it yourself. I find it inadvisable to catch one's own birds in the hand or in a net. Research has shown that birds will remain, for a long time (perhaps even into the breeding season) afraid of a person who has caught them in cage or aviary. I catch my colleagues' birds and they do the same for me. I always wear gloves, as a frightened cockatiel can sometimes give a painful nip; some fanciers have learned the hard way just how powerful a cockatiel's beak can be. For the rest, the above does not mean that the cockatiel is a naturally shy bird. However, they have no sympathy toward someone who has caught them with the hand or in a net, and they remember for a long time the person who did the "bad deed." It is easy to understand that this can lead to a bad breeding season.

Choosing Breed Stock

Cockatiels that one intends to breed must be in top condition and at least one year old. When younger birds are bred, there is a good chance that the hen either will lay infertile eggs or will refuse to brood. It is of course possible for a pair or birds eight or nine months old to lay and brood, but often the eggs are laid on the cage or aviary floor and even brooded there. In order to avoid

Long before the start of the breeding season future parents should be made familiar with rearing or egg foods that are commercially available.

A pair of pearl cockatiels in excellent condition before the start of the breeding season.

a similar cage within sight of each other but out of sight (and hearing) of breeding "competitors." After seven to ten days the birds can be placed together in a suitable breeding cage or aviary. (Birds that have had experience in rearing a brood can be placed in a large aviary with other birds.) You will notice that the hen is usually dominant, though in a nonaggressive manner. Hostility will seldom be seen, but the hen will show herself to be the boss, especially in the first few weeks after the introduction. Familiarity soon sets in, and each bird will continually influence the other: if one goes to drink, the other will follow; if one scratches its plumage, the other will follow. (In this context it is interesting to note that a solitary bird will imitate its owner, whom the bird regards as its "partner" or "mate.")

mishaps, it is kindest to remove the eggs and not to supply a nest box. The pair should be separated until they have reached adequate age. Even after the separation the hen might still lay eggs on the floor of her cage. These should be removed and destroyed because they are infertile. Sometimes an older pair that does not have a nest box will lay eggs on the floor and brood them, usually with tragic results. Even if youngsters hatch, they usually die within 24 hours.

Birds ready to breed should be introduced with deliberation. The best method is to place each bird in

The Nest Box

If you have an outdoor aviary, it is best to hang the nest box in the night shelter (see page 29). Wherever possible, offer twice as many nest boxes as there are pairs of birds. Also, it is recommended that all boxes be fixed on the same wall and at the same height in order to avoid minor squabbles. Leave enough room between the nest box and the top of the cage or night shelter so that birds that are not brooding can sit on top of the nest box—a favored position at this time.

A clutch is the term used for all of the eggs laid and brooded (incubated) by a bird during a single incubation period.

Welcome to this world!

As we already know, cockatiels in the wild do not construct a nest as such, but use a hollow in a thick branch or tree trunk (see page 165). In captivity, however, cockatiels use a nest box. The floor area is best 10 by 10 inches (25.5 × 25.5 cm), the height 12 inches (30 cm), and an entrance hole with a diameter of about 3½ inches (9 cm), placed about 2½ inches (6.5 cm) below the roof. Cockatiels are not fussy about the form of their nursery, and you can use old (but not warped) wood about ¾ inch (1.9 cm) thick to construct nest boxes that should last for many years. Just below the entrance hole, fix a perch 7 inches (18 cm) long and about ⅝ inch (1.6 cm) in diameter, so that it protrudes both inside and outside the nest box. The box's floor can be covered with a 1½- to 2-inch (4–5-cm) layer of damp peat mixed with a few wood shavings. In the middle of this layer, press a hollow with your fist to create a place where the hen can later place her eggs. This depression prevents the egg from rolling around too much. There are nest boxes available commercially that have a removable board complete with a hollow for this purpose. One disadvantage of such a board is that the eggs tend to dry out.

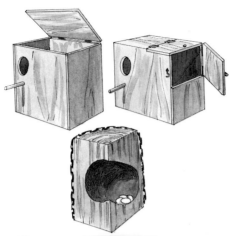

Wooden nest boxes are the most common breeding quarters. They must provide ample space as cock and hen are often in the nest box together, especially when the weather is cold or after the young are hatched and asking for food.

The oil or preen gland is a small nipple-like organ located beneath the rump at the base of the tail. It contains an oily substance that is secreted via a duct through an external opening at the surface of the skin. The oily substance is applied to the feathers as a surface coating (aligning of feathers, waterproofing, insulation, etc.). It also lubricates the horny covering of the bill (rhamphotheca), minimizing flaking deterioration.

The inner wall of the nest box below the entrance hole should have a ladder to help the birds climb up and down. This ladder might be made of large staples or wire mesh, for example. One disadvantage of using wire mesh is that, sooner or later, a bird will get its claws or leg band stuck, and will have to be rescued. I personally prefer to use a few large staples or possibly a few pieces of wood nailed to the wall, although these latter will be gradually gnawed away until there is no more ladder! Each nest box should have an inspection door in one of its sides, and the roof should be hinged so that you can inspect the premises easily.

The nest boxes are best installed in the night shelter for the following reasons:

• It is the most peaceful spot; the change of disturbance is minimal.
• There is less chance of untoward occurrences upsetting the birds at night, causing them to panic and leave the nest box, abandoning the eggs.
• The nest box is less likely to be affected by adverse weather conditions, such as late-night frosts, strong sunlight, or driving rain.

Australian parakeets in general, and cockatiels in particular, are certainly not particularly fussy about their nests. You can try to get along with one nest box per pair. (But if the birds show no interest at the beginning of the season, you should hang additional boxes in different spots.) And if you buy young birds for eventual breeding, examine the type of nest box in which they themselves were reared; then make a box similar to that in which the hen was born.

There are two possibilities when the time comes for hanging the nest boxes: to install them so that they can be left in position all year long, or to install them only as the breeding season approaches. Each method has its advantages and disadvantages. If the nest boxes are left in position the whole year (and, of course, they must be thoroughly cleaned after the breeding season), the birds will decide for themselves when they want to breed, as they do in the wild. A disadvantage is the damage that can be caused by low temperatures and late frosts in an outdoor aviary. If you give them the chance, cockatiels will breed the whole year round, something that is not good for them. They must have a good six-month rest period if they are to raise healthy, lively youngsters. Personally, I let my cockatiels breed from the beginning of April through to the middle or even the end of September; in the period from October to March, I give the birds extra food, thus strengthening them so that they will be in peak breeding condition at the beginning of next season. After the breeding season, the birds are somewhat low in weight and usually start their molt. That is the time to remove the nest boxes or at least block the entrance holes. Fanciers who place the nest boxes in position just before the breeding season thus have a greater

What's going on, folks? Why are you here? There is rarely any great variance in the incubation time. The normal range is 19 to 21 days. Temperature, humidity, disturbances (like here!), and other factors may make a difference of a day or so in the time the eggs hatch.

control of the breeding pairs. The proper time for placement depends on the weather and the readiness of the birds.

There are several choices of nest material in addition to the peat mixed with wood shavings already

Indoor breeding is very well possible. This set-up is all "hand-made."

There is the first hatchling! Hatching in ornithology means breaking through and emerging from an eggshell—the first act of a young bird or the final act of a bird embryo.

mentioned. If you keep this mixture damp, there will be no danger; but if it dries out, there is a possibility that the young will contract respiratory problems caused by inhaling dust and fungal spores. In such dry con-

In order to avoid breakage of the eggs, the bottom of the nest box can best be covered with a layer of pine chips, although chances are that the female bird will remove all or part of it.

ditions there is also the possibility that the nostrils can become blocked. I personally like to use a nesting material composed of potting or woodland soil, mixed with a little rotting leaf or needle litter. Other acceptable alternatives include an upturned grass sod with some sawdust pressed in with the fist, rotten wood that the birds can chew up themselves, and wood shavings mixed with chopped corn cobs. Whatever nest material you use must be dampened before you place it in the nest box, and then kept damp (but not wet!), in order to foster healthy development of the eggs—whether in indoor or outdoor aviaries.

The Eggs

If all goes well, the birds will accept the nest box and soon begin mating. The first egg is laid 10 to 14 days after the first pairing. The eggs are usually laid in the afternoon or early evening at intervals of about 48 hours. The eggs vary in number from four to seven and, as Forshaw says, are "broad-elliptical with a slight gloss." The average size is slightly less than 1 inch by ¾ inch (24.5 × 19 mm). The eggs are brooded for 19 to 21 days. As brooding commences after the second or third egg has been laid, the first youngsters hatch together, but the later eggs hatch at intervals of 48 hours. Both cock and hen cockatiels share in the brooding, just like cockatoos.

Some breeders remove the first eggs and replace them when the clutch is complete, so that all youngsters will hatch at about the same time. In my opinion this is not really necessary; in nature there are also differences in size and age, and there is enough food for all young to be reared. However, in large clutches—which are not uncommon—the size difference between the youngest and oldest hatchling can be large, and the youngest can be "left behind."

In any case, if the eggs are removed, they must be turned several times per day. Observations have shown that cockatiels turn their eggs about every half hour during the day and about every one to two hours during the night—approximately 24 turns per day. This prevents the embryo from adhering to the albumen in the egg, which could be fatal. Eggs should not be stored at too high a temperature as the embryo will begin to develop. The eggs can be marked with a soft pencil to identify them with date of laying and other information. Ink or felt-tipped pens should not be used.

Eggs that have been incubated for a minimum of five days can be tested for fertility by shining a flashlight through them. A fertile egg will show red veins through the shell as they grow out around the yolk. Infertile eggs are translucent. However, do not be in too much of a hurry to dispose of apparently infertile eggs—the hen may not have brooded as long as you think. Infer-

Mating cockatiels.

tile eggs also have a use in the nest; they hold warmth and offer some support for the fertile eggs.

There are various reasons why eggs are infertile: infertile birds; parents that are too young to be in full breeding condition; incompatible pairs; or an overly aggressive hen, though this is uncommon. If a little hole or dent appears, the egg will be subject to desiccation. You can help by painting a tiny bit of colorless nail polish over the blemish. This will close off the hole and prevent desiccation if you do it in time.

Some birds are egg eaters. There is not much you can do about this except to take each egg away as soon as it is laid, replacing it with an artificial egg (which you can obtain from a bird society or from a pet shop). You can also take an egg that you know is infertile, smear it with a mixture of hot mustard and pepper,

The number of cockatiel eggs may vary from four to seven. They are white and elliptical with a slight gloss.

Any eggs that for some reason or other cannot be left with the hen can be stored for a few days. Tests on cockatiel eggs have shown that the chances of fertility begin to decrease after three days and that the situation becomes really serious after six days. It is therefore advisable to put the eggs in an incubator; what happens thereafter depends on various factors.

The best thing to do, of course, is to replace the eggs under the mother as quickly as possible. If this is not possible, you must try to find suitable foster parents that are themselves brooding at the time. Different species can be used, but the difference in size between the birds should not be too great. Various species are suitable as foster parents for cockatiels, including, for example, the yellow-fronted parakeet *(Cyanorhamphus auriceps),* the red-fronted parakeet *(C. novaezelandae),* and the red-rumped parakeet *(Psephotus haematonus).* If you do not have suitable foster parents in your own aviary, perhaps your bird fancier colleagues can help out.

and place it in the nest. The offensive taste may cause the bird to change its ways. It sometimes happens that the problem disappears once the hen starts brooding; then you must find the right moment to replace the original eggs.

It would be advantageous to use a nest box with a removable base with a concave bottom so the eggs don't have a chance to roll to all the corners of the box.

The last possibility is to allow the eggs to hatch in the incubator and to hand-rear the youngsters yourself. This can be a difficult and time-consuming task. At first, the youngsters must be fed every two hours, including nights. Thus, at least for a few weeks, you will be totally committed every day, and you must arrange your time to suit the babies. The food itself should not pose too many problems, since there are various mixtures available on the market. For more detailed information, see page 73.

Clearly, however, youngsters reared by their natural parents will be healthier and better off than orphans. In feeding and behavior, the real parents can offer more than we can.

Now, a little about the viability of male sperm cells. Each egg is not specially fertilized. Birds copulate frequently—nature's way of ensuring that all the hen's eggs are fertilized. In addition, the male's sperm stays fertile in the hen's body for days, sometimes weeks. Thus, even if the cock, for one reason or another, is no longer with the hen, the eggs can be fertile. I had such an experience with a pair of normal gray cockatiels. It so happened that the cock became sick after the first egg was laid, and I had to separate him from the hen. The hen then laid another four eggs. From the total clutch of five, the last four eggs were fertile.

There is rarely any great variance in the incubation time (19–21 days). Temperature, humidity, and other factors can all influence the incubation time, however, and may make a difference of a day more or less in the time the eggs hatch.

The Nestlings

As most cockatiels begin to breed at the beginning of April, most nestlings fledge in June and July. The time between the first egg and

Two-and-a-half-week-old chicks.

fledgling is approximately two months. The eggs are not brooded for the first few days; then a brooding period of about 20 days follows.

After the young hatch, the parents (the hen, in particular) hardly leave the nest box for a few days, as the hatchlings cannot yet keep themselves warm. A newly hatched chick weighs approximately two thirds the weight of its egg. The youngster will have enough food in the yolk sac to keep it going for a while, so it does not require immediate feeding.

If you breed your birds indoors under artificial light, you must ensure that the birds have light for a long enough period each day to ensure that the hen has adequate time to feed her offspring before "lights out." However, there is not really much point in having light for more than 14 hours each day. Do not turn off the light suddenly. If you do, and if a brooding hen or a hen with newly hatched young is out of the nest when the light is turned off, the brood will suffer because their mother may not be able to find her way back to the nest box in the dark. Therefore, use a dimmer and, ideally, leave on a 7-watt night light during the hours of darkness. By the way, the eyes of the nestlings open after about one week.

Banding

You may band the birds' legs between the sixth and tenth days, depending on their size. There are two methods of banding; the first is over the two front toes and then over the two rear toes; the second is to hold the two front toes and the longer one of the rear toes to the front, leaving the shorter rear toe to the rear. Although the joint may be thicker in the second method, I find it the easiest way. The advantage is that the diameter of the band is just a little greater than the joint. It is rather difficult to pass the band over the long rear toe—as in the first method—especially if you are a little late with the banding. A closed band for a cockatiel should be about $\frac{3}{16}$ of an inch (5.4 mm) in diameter.

Once the band is on the leg, test it to see if it slides off; if it does, wait a couple of days and then do the banding again. A great advantage of leg banding is that you are able to identify individual birds without having to catch them. For example, if you have two pairs of birds, band the young from the first pair on the left leg and those from the second pair on the right. You can then easily select an unrelated pair for further breeding.

Once hatched, the young stay about 35 days in the nest. Like all other parrot-like birds, cockatiels are very nest-dependent; this means that the young must be fed by the parents for a relatively long period before they become independent.

The parents will normally rear their youngsters themselves without problems, provided you give them an adequate diet. When the youngsters finally come out of the nest box, they will be a bit wild and nervous. Actually, this is to be expected, considering how new and unknown everything is to them. When they first enter the flight, they may fly against the wire mesh, since they will not be able to distinguish it or even know what it is. Before the birds fledge, therefore, it is a good idea to place twigs or sacking against the wire. Further, ensure that the birds are all in the shelter at night; an encounter with a cat or an owl in the night can have fatal consequences.

The youngsters will be fed by the parents for some time even after they leave the nest box. The young birds have to learn slowly how to feed themselves and should therefore be left with the parents at least three weeks—a little longer will do no harm. However, when the parents are ready to start a new brood, they will become aggressive toward the young.

Fledgling cockatiels have a juvenile plumage. They molt for the first time in the fall (juvenile molt), after which they get their adult plumage. A smooth-running juvenile molt is important if the youngsters are to be fully prepared for the inclement weather of late fall and winter.

Trouble-shooting

The breeding process is not always without problems. In trying to find out why something has gone wrong, do not immediately place all of the blame on the birds. Examine the circumstances and try to find out the cause by asking yourself the following questions:
• Have I bought birds of the best quality?
• Are the birds in breeding condition?
• Have the birds had adequate time to accustom themselves to their new home and to each other?
• Do I really have a true pair, a cock and a hen? (Do not forget that the sexes are difficult to distinguish in some of the color mutations.)
• Do I feed the birds an adequate, balanced diet?
• Do they have adequate nesting facilities?
• Are they exposed to only the minimum disturbance?

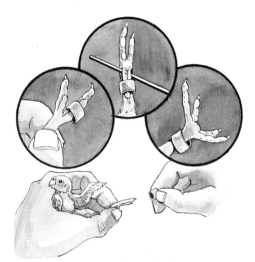

Banding a nine-day-old chick; clockwise, from the bottom: preparing to slip the band on; the two front toes enclosed by the band; after you push the band down, the two back toes are pulled out with a toothpick; the band is in place.

• Are there aggressive, bothersome birds in the aviary?

If you can truthfully say that the answers to the above questions do not give a clue to the failure, have a little patience and allow your birds another chance next season. Don't hastily dispose of your birds and acquire new ones; not every pair breeds at the word of command. In fact, this is a good thing; otherwise the hobby would have no challenges and would lose its attraction for many. In fact, you are a real bird fancier only if you can, after each breeding season and after each winter, continue to be happy with your hobby in spite of any setbacks you may have had.

Pointers for Breeders

- Cockatiels that are kept in roomy aviaries or large breeding cages are likely to want to rear brood after brood. In such cases, it is wise to remove the nest boxes. Your birds should not be allowed to rear more than three broods per season. As the third brood fledges, watch out for the next clutch; these eggs should be removed and disposed of as soon as the clutch is complete.
- It is possible to breed cockatiels in a colony. In fact, some fanciers get better results when they keep three or four pairs together. Of course, the pairs should all be placed in the aviary at the same time. The birds should all be mature, and there should be more nest boxes than pairs of birds. Be absolutely sure that you have equal numbers of cocks and hens.
- Cockatiels can reach an age of 25 years; hens can lay eggs for 8 to 10 years, but these decrease in fertility as the bird gets older; cocks can remain fertile for 12 to 14 years.
- The young produce a great quantity of droppings in the nest box, so it is wise to have an absorbent nesting material in place. It should not be too fine, as discussed earlier (page 123); otherwise the young may be subject to respiratory problems.
- It can also happen that the parents will feed the young too much green food, for example, and the droppings will be extremely wet and likely to soil the developing plumage. In such cases you should add additional absorbent material to the nest box.
- You should also examine the youngsters' toes regularly and, if necessary, clean them, removing the hard "bobbles" on the end of each toe. Otherwise, the birds will be unable to climb the ladder to escape the box at fledgling time.
- During the breeding season, the birds must have facilities for bathing. During warm weather, the hens in particular will make good use of the bath.
- With regard to temperature, the newly fledged young must be kept inside the shelter when outside temperatures are cold.
- The proper diet is especially important during the breeding season. I give my birds, young and old, mineralized grit, oyster shell grit, and cuttlebone. I also give wheat bread soaked in milk to all pairs while they are brooding and rearing. But this must be given in fresh batches regularly, especially during warm weather, as it will quickly turn sour. Uneaten bread should be removed before this happens. I also give seeding dandelions and chickweed, which I grow in special pots. I do not collect this green food from the wild because chickweed can harbor the eggs of the threadworm *Capillaria*. From the garden you can, without danger, give the heads of forget-me-nots, while wild honeysuckle flowers are a healthful delicacy—my birds gobble them up!

Worming the Fledglings

When the young cockatiels reach ten weeks of age, they must be wormed. They require half the dosage of that recommended for adult birds (see page 116), and they can be given this dose until they are five months old, after which they can receive the adult dosage. It is best to obtain the services of someone to hold the bird when you are administering vermicidal medicines. (And don't forget to wear gloves to protect yourself from the bird's beak.) There are various worming compounds available on the market. An excellent medicine is Fenbendazole, a white fluid that is administered to each bird at the dosage recommended by your avian veterinarian. Fenbendazole is a slow-working drug, so it may take several days after treatment before all worms have been destroyed. The veterinarian may also supply Panacur (which contains Fenbendazole). Panacur is made in two strengths; I use the 2.5 solution without trace additives. Take 5 grams of Panacur and suspend it in grenadine (or any other simple syrup). Bring the total amount of fluid to 20 cc. One gram of Panacur is a little more than a normal, flat teaspoonful. Since each cc contains 20 drops, 20 cc is good for approximately 400 drops. Before and during use the mixture must be thoroughly shaken as the Panacur powder sinks. The only disadvantage of this medicine is that it will not keep for more than a few months, at which time a fermentary process spoils it. Unopened Panacur will last for one year. I personally buy a new supply each year as it is not expensive. Consult your veterinarian for the proper dosage.

Administer the drops directly into the beak with a syringe or pipette. Do not be concerned if you give your pet a slight overdose. Insert the nozzle of the syringe into the side of the beak. (Some fanciers like to place a 2-inch [5-cm] tube over the nozzle; the tube is then passed a short distance down the throat). Be very careful not to squirt the medicine, as it could then be forced into the lungs, a possibly fatal mistake! Wait until the bird is fully relaxed before administering the medicine.

Beginners to the hobby are often afraid to carry out such treatments; however, you should be able to find an aviculturist in your area who is experienced in worming techniques. One word of advice: suggest to your society that they invite a veterinarian or experienced fancier to give a worming demonstration at one of your meetings.

Chronology

• At about ten days of age, young cockatiels will start to make hissing noises whenever they are disturbed. Each time you inspect the nest, for example, they will hiss as they sway comically and raise their stumpy little crests. (We can also observe this

Cockatiel chicks in an incubator waiting to be hand-fed. At this time youngsters start to hiss at you when they feel threatened.

behavior in adults; sometimes they will spit and spread their tiny wingfeather stumps.)

• At 18–20 days of age, the orange cheek patch will appear in the normal grays and the color mutations that have it. The crest feathers will have grown.

• After 27–32 days the young will look very much like their parents and weigh about 3 ounces (80 g).

• On or about their 35th day, the young will fledge and spend their first day on the ground, with crouched body, looking "questioningly" up for their parents and the prospect of food.

This is the time for fanciers to prepare separate living quarters for the youngsters. As soon as the birds can feed independently (about two to two and one half weeks after fledging), they should be moved to separate quarters. If you breed in cages, you should have one or two large cages placed next to the breeding cage to serve as flights. It is important that the young birds have plenty of room for exercise. As in the aviary, you should place twigs against the cage wire to prevent the fledglings from crashing into it. Since the birds will be in strange surroundings, do not clutter up the area with all manner of utensils that could be dangerous. Use a number of good drinking and feeding containers—open dishes as well as hoppers—some shallow bathing dishes, and adequate perches of varying thicknesses in order to help the birds develop their foot muscles. On these perches they will stretch their wings a lot, so the cage or aviary must not be too narrow.

• After about three weeks, you will notice that the birds are independent. They will no longer beg for food from the parents, but will find it on their own.

Caring for Young Cockatiels

If one of the parents dies during the rearing of a brood, the remaining parent can usually rear the brood adequately, whatever the age of the "orphans." It is a hard task for the single parent, of course, especially when the young have fledged and have positioned themselves in various parts of the aviary. However, the single parent knows the area and can cope with the situation surprisingly well. Occasionally it may happen that one of the parents dies when *very* young hatchlings are in the nest. In this case, you should keep a good eye on the brood. If you think they are getting too cold, place an infrared lamp directed at the nest box from a distance of about 9 to 10 feet (3 m). Test to see that the heat in the box is not too intense by putting your hand in the box now and again. Also, look regularly to see if the crops of the young are adequately filled; if not, you may have to resort to hand-feeding (see page 136).

Even under normal circumstances—that is, when both parents are feeding the young—it can happen that one of the youngsters is suddenly not provided with food. This is Mother Nature's way of showing that a bird is not 100 percent healthy—a natural selection. In cage or aviary this bird is not necessarily sick but for some reason or other is simply being neglected. The best thing to do is to take the neglected bird out of the cage or aviary and to hand-rear it for three or four days. When the "outcast" has caught up with its brothers and sisters, it can then often be returned to the brood with no further problems.

You must be alert for problems. It may happen that some newly fledged youngsters suddenly are unable to fly, even though they may have done so perfectly well at first. This seems to have something to do with a vitamin deficiency, which can be cleared up by adding a good bird vitamin/mineral preparation to the birds' food and water, following the manufacturer's instructions. You can also place a few drops in the throat of each bird. After a few days, they should be back to normal.

Cockatiels are one of the few parrot species that, if kept in a roomy aviary, will tolerate the young of a previous brood when rearing a second. Of course, the aviary must be of sufficient size. The youngsters will generally not hinder their breeding parents. I have occasionally seen that youngsters from an earlier brood will continue to beg from their parents when there is another brood to be fed, but this presents no real problem. It is necessary, however, to keep an eye on the enthusiastic father, so that he does not pair with one of his daughters. In such a case it is best to remove all the female youngsters from the aviary. If the cock should be seen pairing with one of his daughters, do not worry too much. The young hen is not old enough to lay eggs.

If you have any difficulty in distinguishing between the sexes—a common problem when you have color mutations—you must be aware of the following: As the birds become independent, but before the first molt, the males will begin to sing. They hold their heads high, with erect crests, and emit a shrill, somewhat husky series of twitterings. The females do not perform in these concerts, which can go on for half an hour or more! If you have birds for sale, this "competition" can be put to good use, since you can say with certainty which sex a bird is.

Abandoned Eggs

Birds that are too young or inexperienced sometimes fail in the execution of their brooding duties. Also, a hen can die after laying eggs, one of the partners may not share in brooding, and other problems can develop. If you cannot find suitable foster parents (including, perhaps, those that belong to a friend) to continue the brooding process, it is advisable to have an incubator available. The artificial incubation of eggs poses no difficulties, but the hand-feeding of the newly hatched young is a great consumer of time, often taxing one's patience and resulting in many sleepless nights!

The Incubator

There are various kinds of incubators available, but the so-called forced air incubator is the best type for the aviculturist. There are various makes and prices. A good incubator is the Marsh-Lyon Model T.S.1 Water Thermostat Unit (made by Lyon Electric Company of San Diego, California). The primary requirement for an incubator, whatever the make, should be that it has an efficient thermostat.

The incubator should be placed on a good solid base in an area where temperature fluctuations are minimal. If the incubator is placed in a sunny position, in no time at all it could become an oven. The thermostat should be set at 99.5°F (37.5°C) with a humidity of 68 percent. Before placing water in the incubator, check the room's humidity, which is frequently higher than you might think, especially in states like Florida, where the relative humidity runs higher than average. The higher the humidity outside the incubator, the smaller the amount of water in the incubator reservoir.

The Egg Candler

In addition to an incubator, it is recommended that you acquire an egg candler to use in inspecting the eggs for fertility. A strong flashlight will also do the job. Hold the egg carefully with thumb and forefinger, or on a transparent egg spoon, and shine a flashlight on the shell. If the egg is fertile, you will see a circular red spot (the embryo) with blood vessels radiating out from it. I have heard some fanciers refer to this as resembling a spider's web, with a fat spider in the center. An infertile egg will not have this spot.

Incubating Eggs

Eggs placed in an incubator should be inspected for little cracks or dents. Eggs that are smeared with droppings should not be washed as even more pores can be blocked with bacteria. In serious cases, very fine sandpaper can help, but this is not without great risks, including total breakage of the egg. In general, dirty eggs do not pose problems, and I clean them only in exceptional circumstances. Tiny cracks or dents can be repaired with clear nail polish.

When eggs have been abandoned for a time (especially those that come from an outdoor aviary), they will most likely be cold. Do not put such eggs directly into the incubator, but place them on a cottonwood "bed" in a small box and keep them in the room where the incubator is kept. After a few hours, place the eggs in the incubator. If all goes well, the incubation period will be 17–22 days. For obvious reasons, you should keep a record of the times, and when the seventeenth day arrives, you must be especially alert for the eggs to hatch. Ten days after placing eggs in the incubator, I candle them to see if any are infertile. I mark the infertile eggs and test them again four days later; if they are still infertile, I dispose of them.

To prevent infections, eggs should always be handled with clean hands. Also, avoid holding the eggs over the candler for too long a time. The heat generated can be dangerous for the growing embryo. After the sixteenth day, do not turn the eggs any longer, and increase the amount of water in the incubator to ensure that the humidity is kept above 70 percent. Research has shown that this makes "pipping" (hatching) easier.

Pipping

You can observe the wonder of hatching from close quarters, as all incubators that I am familiar with have a transparent lid. If an active chick with a pink to red body emerges, you have a healthy bird. Some hatchlings are out of the egg in no time at all, while others may take up to 40 hours to emerge. If it takes longer than 40 hours, make a close examination but do not be too quick to intervene. If you act too early, the youngster could die. If the new hatchling looks pale and white, with a bit of yolk still attached to its belly, you were too early, and such a chick is doomed. If you suspect an embryo is weak, do not bother to help it hatch. A bird too weak to hatch normally may live a day or two, but will then die anyway.

Suppose you have an egg from which you suspect a chick is unable to liberate itself. The days of brooding have passed, and the egg should be ready to hatch. You are expecting a totally healthy youngster to emerge, but nothing happens. In such a case, I follow the approach of budgie expert Gerald S. Binks, described in his fascinating book *Best in Show*. He has prepared a table to guide the decision on whether to assist or stand by (see chart, page 136).

Binks suggests laying the egg in question on a prewarmed, thick bath towel, with the part of the egg that has been cracked the most facing you. Cut a circle around the crack with a sharpened wooden matchstick. Be sure to cut through the membrane under the shell. You will see a little blood in the process, but

Deciding Whether to Assist or Stand By

Sound	Appearance	Action
Quiet tapping	1/16-inch crack	Too soon—replace
Quiet tapping	Group of fine cracks	Too soon—replace
Quiet tapping	Cracks plus brown line	Too soon—replace
Weak squeaks	Cracks plus tiny hole	Too soon—replace
Medium squeaks	Cracks and early discoloration	Too soon—replace
Loud squeaks	Crack line around circumference—creamy patches, moist membrane	Normal hatching—replace
Loud squeaks	Crack line around circumference—creamy patches, dried membrane	Assist
Loud squeaks	Large hole—drying membrane	Assist

if your timing is right and everything else goes as planned, you have assisted in bringing a healthy chick into the world (see page 134).

Hand-rearing

The Brooder

As soon as the young have hatched, transfer them from the incubator to the brooder. Such a brooder can be a hospital cage, an old aquarium, or a glass-fronted wooden box. The brooder should be heated from above with two 60-watt bulbs. At first, maintain the temperature at a constant 99.5°F (37.5°C). As the young mature, lower the temperature gradually, but do not reduce below 86°F (30°C). Only when they are independent enough to be housed in an outside aviary can the young be acclimatized to lower temperatures.

Ideally, the temperature in the brooder should be controlled with a good thermostat, as sudden temperature changes cannot be tolerated by young nestlings. As the birds grow larger, they will, now and again, move out of the main heat source—this will do them no harm.

Feeding

There is no point in preparing your own rearing food. There are various good hand-rearing foods on the market; all come with instructions. Most formulas just require the addition of warm (100–108°F [37.7–42.2°C]) bottled (*not* distilled) water. To feed these formulas use a plastic eye dropper or syringe or—my personal favorite—a teaspoon with its sides bent inward.

When you see newly hatched cockatiels, you will realize just how small and soft their beaks are, especially compared to the feeding utensils you are going to use. If you gently tap the top of the beak with a little spoon, the youngster will frequently gape—that is, open its beak. If the bird does not open up, you must, with great care, open the beak with a pointed matchstick. As soon as the beak is open, drop a tiny drop of water into the throat. The bird will swallow the drop of water. After a few trials, the bird will know what is happening and will open its beak each time you "tickle" it with a feeding utensil.

A group of young cockatiels.

When to Feed: The newly hatched chick requires no food for the first 10 to 15 hours. Thereafter, start with one drop of lukewarm water; after one hour, another drop with some pulverized, clean (meaning pure white) cuttlebone and pure yogurt; after another hour, another such drop. Thereafter, feed a few drops of very thin hand-rearing diet every hour. Once a day I mix in a little yogurt because it contains vitamin K, the blood-clotting vitamin. Vitamin K can also be obtained from some grains and soybeans, which is usually included in rearing food, so it is not absolutely necessary to include yogurt. Nevertheless, even though yogurt is not the birds' favorite food, I like to give it as a supplement. I have also had success with the major hand-rearing diets that are commercially available. (For more information see my

It is advisable to weigh each hand-reared chick before and after each feeding. Always determine the fullness of the chick's crop and stop feeding when the food starts flowing back into the mouth.

A cinnamon and pearl pied baby.

book, *Hand-Feeding and Raising Baby Birds*.)

The following is an outline of the feeding schedule from day 4 to day 25:

• Days 4–9: Feed every two hours though no feeding need take place between midnight and 5:00 A.M. The formula must have the consistency of creamy milk.

• Days 10–14: Feed every three hours from 5:00 A.M. to midnight. Consistency as indicated above.

• Days 15–20: Feed every four hours in slightly thicker formula than above. After 20 days, birds must be housed in a cage with low perches and a shallow bowl of water. As young birds of this age are very curious and will peck at everything on the ground or on the wire, it is recommended that you offer the following "snacks": well-washed twigs of willow, hazel, or apple, cut into 1-inch (2.5-cm) lengths; crushed canary grass seed; pulverized cuttlebone (clean and white!); some egg food; and millet spray, which should be dunked in boiling water to kill any potential disease organisms.

• Days 21–25: Feed hand-rearing formulas two or three times during the day. Use same formula consistency, but introduce free choice of sprouted seeds and millet spray (fresh and not scalded), to encourage the baby birds to forage on their own. Mix some dry formula with the soaked seeds. Also give egg food, cuttlebone powder, chopped fruits and vegetables, and fine grit.

The hand-reared youngsters will be very tame and affectionate. After all, they see their hand-rearer as their parent! Moreover, hand-reared birds are good for breeding; they are almost certain to bring strong offspring into the world!

How to Feed: Add warm (100–108°F [37.7–42.2°C]) bottled (*not* distilled) water or apple juice to the formula. Mix well until it has the consistency of creamy milk. Never administer the formula too thick, as it will congeal in the bird's crop and be unable to pass into the stomach. By giving the baby bird lukewarm water and gently massaging the crop you should be able to correct this problem. If the crop remains full, however, or if it is not emptying correctly, there could be a digestive problem; consult an avian veterinarian or an experienced birdbreeder immediately!

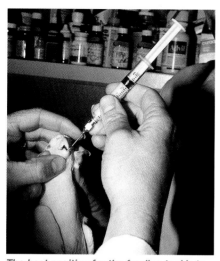

The best position for the feeding tool is to the left of the baby bird's beak angled down to the right, hence next to your left hand.

Syringe feeding. The temperature of the formula (and there are excellent ready-to-use hand-feeding diets commercially available) should be between 100–108°F (37.7–42.2°C).

Draw formula into the plastic eyedropper or syringe, or let it roll off a teaspoon, the sides of which have been bent inwards—as mentioned, this is the utensil I like best. All feeding implements should be as close to the temperature of the formula as possible: 100–108°F (37.7–42.2°C).

Use only one feeding instrument and one feeding dish for each baby bird; never dip a feeding instrument into the food dish of another baby bird after it has touched the first baby bird's mouth. Sterilize your feeding instruments after feeding.

Maintain the right temperature for the formula during the whole feeding process by placing the dish with bird formula in a pan of warm (100–108°F [37.7–42.2°C]) water.

Place the baby bird on a flat surface on a hand-warmed bath towel and support the bird with a cupped (and warmed!) hand. When the baby bird doesn't want to open its beak (gape), tap the beak gently with the feeding utensil.

Examine the bird's crop before each feeding in order to determine the frequency and volume of feeding. Remember, a crop should never become completely empty. Usually the crop will empty itself in three and one half to four hours. However, don't overfill the crop, which could lead to a backflow up the gullet (esophagus), into the throat, and down the windpipe, possibly resulting in death! Stop feeding immediately if the food begins flowing back into the mouth. Don't resume feeding until the mouth is completely empty.

Feeding has to be synchronized with swallowing. As soon as the

Spoon-feeding young cockatiels. Hand-feeding is also done with a syringe.

baby bird swallows, which is accompanied by a rhythmic bobbing of the head, deliver the formula quickly. Place the feeding device in the mouth over the tongue.

After each feeding, rinse the inside of the bird's mouth with a few drops of warm (100–108°F [37.7–42.2°C]) water. Also, clean the bird's beak, head, and other parts, as well as the anus (vent) with lukewarm water, and then return the baby bird to its warm brooder.

Chapter Seven
Heredity and Mutations

During the last few years, the breeding of color mutations in cockatiels has attracted a great deal of attention. It would be a shortcoming not to cover this exciting new branch of the hobby, especially as interest in mutations is rapidly increasing.

While it will not be possible to delve deeply into the subject of genetics, I will try to explain the essential principles as simply and practically as possible. Note well, however, that some time and patience will be required of anyone who has not previously studied the subject.

Colors

Three factors produce all of the color variants seen in psittacines: changes in the pigment melanin; changes in the pigment carotenoid; changes in the structure color blue.

Melanin: the dark pigments of the feathers, eyes, beak, feet, and nails—in other words, the colors black, gray, and brown.

Carotenoid: the bright pigments, which can occur in feathers and beak—specifically the colors yellow, orange, and red.

Structure Color: blue (and violet). The words *structure color* indicate that the color is related to the *structure* of the feather. In other words, blue plumage is not the result of a distinctive pigment; rather, it is a physical effect produced by the structural arrangement of molecules on the feather's surface.

This is one of the later mutations—a white, not an albino, female cockatiel with black instead of red eyes (as in albinos); this mutation is autosomal recessive.

The breeding of color mutations in cockatiels has become a major part of aviculture. It obviously all started with the domesticated wild-colored or normal gray birds—after they were being bred in captivity some 100 years after they were first introduced to Europe!

A lutino mutation. Some lutino birds have a visible bald patch at the back of the head. This is a genetic fault that has so far not been bred out.

Right a pied, left a pearl pied cockatiel.

A champion heavy pied cockatiel, bred and owned by the author.

You will have noticed that the color green has not been mentioned. This is because green, which is not a primary color, results from a combination of the carotenoid pigment color yellow and the structure color blue. If the yellow fails in a green bird, the result is a blue bird; if the blue fails, the result is a yellow one.

Mutations

Mutations in the psittacine species are generally caused by changes in the melanin and the carotenoid, and only occasionally in the structure color. We can therefore concern ourselves mainly with the changes in melanin and carotenoid. The following are the most usual forms. (Note that not all of these color mutations have been observed in cockatiels, though it remains theoretically possible that they may occur in the future.)

Pastel: In this mutation, the quantity of melanin is reduced. The colors of the wild form are retained in lighter, diluted form—frequently as light, grass green. The yellow turquoisine parakeet is an example of this mutation.

Lutino, Albino, Yellow: In these mutations, melanin is completely or almost completely lacking. In lutinos and albinos, melanin is absent from all parts of the body—feathers, eyes, beak, feet, and nails. In yellows, melanin is absent only from the plumage. Lutinos and albinos are therefore easily recognizable by their

A male lutino pied cockatiel.

red eyes; normal yellows have dark eyes. Lutinos and albinos differ from each other in that the former still has its carotenoid and, therefore, will show some yellow, orange, and/or red, while the latter has lost these colors as well as the melanin colors, leaving a pure white bird with red eyes.

In cockatiels, lutino males are whitish with buttercup yellow suffusion, especially under the wings and tail, red-orange cheek patches, dark red eyes, pinkish feet and legs, and horn-gray beak and yellow crest. The females are like the cocks. Barring on the undersurfaces of the tail and underwing feathers appear to be yellow against a white background, due to the lack of melanin. The young are like the females, but the eyes are lighter with some yellow. This mutation originated in 1958 in Florida from two normal-looking cockatiels, in the aviaries of Mr. C. Barringer. It was, however, the late Mrs. E. L. Moon who saw to it that this mutation was firmly established. In the lutino cockatiel the melanin has been lost completely, although the red cheek patches are retained.

Since albino cockatiels are void of all carotenoid, both sexes are pure white with ruby or red eyes; even the orange-red ear patches are white. Primaries and flight feathers have sometimes an off shade of white. The albino mutation occurred in the Netherlands in the early 1980s.

Pied, Opaline: Here, the melanin is absent from parts of the plumage. The pied mutation usually has a patchy, irregular color pattern, with white or yellow patches where the melanin is absent. There is a great variety of pied patterns, ranging from a few affected feathers to large areas of the plumage.

In cockatiels, pied males are like normal gray cocks, but with irregular white patches—which may be small, large, or between these extremes. Ideal pied mutations are clear (meaning: without melanin). Eyes brown, feet and legs grayish, beak gray. Females are like normal gray hens, but with the plumage broken by white patches. The tail is usually clear without bars. The warbling whistle of the male may be the best—and often only—indication of the bird's sex. The young have shorter tails and often some pink

around the cere. This mutation originated in the United States in 1949. Different strains were developed in the aviaries of Mr. D. Putman and Mrs. R. Kersh. Birds of the latter were used to found European strains. Females can be split to pied as the mutation is recessive; split birds often have white or yellow flecked feathers on the back of the neck.

This mutation must not be confused with the results of an inadequate diet. A deficiency of the amino acid lysine in the diet, for example, can result in an inadequate formation of melanin. Thus, some green feathers can become yellow, while black ones can become very pale gray to whitish. An improvement in the diet will result in normalization of the plumage after the following molt.

The second mutation in this category is the opaline. Here, the carotenoid becomes more intense. Light yellow becomes deep yellow, medium yellow becomes near orange, and pink becomes near red. The opaline mutation is difficult to recognize, as its outward appearance varies from species to species. I will, therefore, provide short descriptions of three "typical" opalines: the red rosella, the rose Bourke's, and the pearled cockatiel.

In the red rosella, virtually the whole underside and tail are red; red can also be seen in the back markings.

The rose Bourke's is also a brilliant example of the opaline mutation. The normal yellowish color is replaced by a pure pink, and the melanin is lost in the mantel, back, secondary flight feathers, and head. This arrangement is similar to that of the budgerigar, in which the mantel has no markings; in the Bourke's this also applies to part of the wings.

The pearled (or opaline) cockatiel shows a totally different variation. Melanin is absent from the center of the feather, so that each affected feather is white or yellow with a dark edge. This gives a checkered effect, seen most often on the wings. The yellow of the pearled is lighter than that of a normal gray cockatiel. Birds with a deep yellow color are known as golden pearls. Cockatiels with heavy pearl markings with an elongated effect right down from the back of the neck are known as Laced or Lacewings.

Young cockatiel males are like normal gray cocks. The back of the neck, mantle, and wings are covered with white or yellow pearly markings. After approximately 6–12 months, the males molt into their adult plumage, being normal gray. The hens, however, keep their beautiful pearling. Eyes, beak, feet, and legs are as in normal gray. This mutation was first seen in 1967 in West Germany and the next year in Belgium. The pearled mutation has been used for breeding and establishing the so-called double and combined mutations (Cinnamon-Pearl, Pearl Pied, Lutino Pearl, Lutino Pearl Pied, and so on).

Cinnamon, Fallow: In these mutations, the color of the melanin is changed: black is replaced by brown. In cinnamons (usually called Isabelles in Europe), brown predominates; fallows show a gray-brown that is particularly obvious on the primary wing feathers.

These mutations give varying outward appearances, depending on the bird species. The effects are more obvious in a cockatiel than in a Bourke's or a kakariki. Green becomes lighter in color and more yellowish; gray becomes more brown-gray.

Male cockatiels are like normal gray cocks, but with a warm tannish (brownish) tone; after the first molt cocks acquire dark rather than barred

A beautiful cinnamon pearl male cockatiel.

Left, a male and right, a female pearl cockatiel.

A pearl female cockatiel. Males scarcely reveal any pearl design.

undertail coverts. The yellow colors are soft, the orange-red cheek patches bright and clear. In this mutation the melanin is brown, not black. Sometimes birds have splotches of color on wings and back; some even have markings that are scalloped, and show shading. Those birds are often called marbled cinnamons. The females are like normal gray hens, but the dark areas have a brownish tone. In general, the female is somewhat lighter than the male. The young are like the parents, although young males are often paler. The mutation, first bred in Belgium in the early 1960s, is sex-linked.

An interesting difference between the cinnamon and the fallow is that, although the young of both are hatched with red eyes, the cinnamon gets dark eyes within a week and the fallow retains the red eyes. There can, therefore, be no confusion with yellow mutations, which are hatched with dark eyes. The origin of this mutation in the cockatiel has not been precisely documented. It occurred in the United States as well as in Europe in the early 1970s.

Silver (recessive): Male cockatiels are like normal gray cocks, but the gray color is replaced with metallic silver. Both sexes have red eyes.

Females are like the males, with characteristic differences seen in normal gray hens. The young resemble the normal gray cockatiel, but the basic coloration is metallic silver. This mutation was first developed in the late 1950s in Belgium, and was noted for its poor eyesight and fertility. The mutation is now well established, and is less afflicted with blindness.

A second strain of silver is the Dominant or Dilute Silver. The cockatiel is silvery-pastel with bright cheek patches; the eyes are black, the legs and feet are gray. Youngsters look like normals (wild color), although the yellow color is much stronger and the gray is darker, especially on the head (skull cap) and neck. After the first molt, the males become silver gray, although the depth of the color may differ from very light to normal (wild color), but with a yellowish wash. The skull cap (dark gray) remains.

A third strain is the Double Factor. A Dominant (Dilute) Silver cockatiel has genes that produce two visual effects in either a single or double quantity, defined as single or double factor. The latter is responsible for a further dilution with, as a result, a yellowish-white head and wings and a grayish wash. The eyes are black, the feet and legs are gray.

The mutation was first bred by Mr. T. Cole of Swindon, England in 1986. It is still rather rare in aviculture.

Seagreen: In this mutation, the carotenoid is diminished. The plumage, therefore, shows less yellow, orange, and/or red. In a good

This is a beautiful bird with an even pearl design.

seagreen mutation, the carotenoid is reduced by half. There are variations. Less carotenoid produces a more bluish bird; more carotenoid gives a greener one. An example is the seagreen splendid parakeet.

Blue: A pure blue bird has melanin and, of course, the structure color blue. Since carotenoid is absent, yellow, orange, and red tints are totally missing.

The white face or charcoal cockatiel is also included in this group. Here, too, the yellow and red are missing, but since the wild color is not green, the mutation produces white rather than a blue plumage. In other respects, these cockatiel males and females are like normal grays. The mask area of the cock will be pure white after the first molt. This mutation first appeared in a Dutch collection in 1964, and again in 1978 in Frankfurt, West Germany. The mutation, which is recessive, is now well established, often being combined with other mutations in order to create new strains. Well-known, for example, is the triple split to Cinnamon-Pearl and Pied.

Principles of Heredity

We will now consider the means by which the mutations are inherited. This, in turn, determines what the offspring of various combinations will look like.

Dominant: If one of the parent birds is pure-bred (see Recessive below) for the dominant color, all of the young will take on that color. In other words, the pure-bred dominant suppresses all other colors, even though the offspring carry other colors in their genetic material (or *genes*). Colors hidden in the genes can emerge later in particular pairings. In general, the wild color is dominant. (If two birds are pure-bred for the dominant color, all of the offspring will also be pure-bred for the dominant color.)

Recessive: If two recessive-colored birds are bred, the offspring will also be of the recessive color. However, if a dominant bird is paired

with a recessive bird, all of the young will take on the color of the dominant bird. The recessive color is thus hidden.

Pure-bred (homozygous): A pure-bred bird possesses only the genes for the revealed color. All recessive-colored birds must be pure-bred. Dominant-colored birds, however, may carry a masked gene for a recessive color.

Split (heterozygous): This means a bird of the dominant color has a hidden color mutation, which can be passed on to its offspring. For example, a green bird with a hidden blue mutation in its genetic makeup is called "split for blue" or "green/blue."

Sex-linked: This means that the inheritance of a particular factor is dependent on sex. For example, hemophilia in humans is carried by females, but is revealed only in males. It is thus important to know which cockatiel parent has the appropriate colors that, with the sex, will be passed on to the young.

Sex-linked recessive means that the recessive gene for a particular factor is associated with the group of genes (or *chromosomes*) that determines the sex of the offspring.

Autosomal: This refers to inheritance that is not sex-linked.

Autosomal recessive means that the gene for the factor in question is not carried on a sex chromosome.

In most cases, the same mutations are inherited by the same means, although there are occasional exceptions to the rules. One example is the lutinos: most inherit sex-linked recessive, but there are also some lutino forms that inherit autosomal recessive (the lutino Princess of Wales parakeet and the lutino elegant parakeet, for example).

Formulas

Most color mutations in cockatiels may be dealt with either in the autosomal recessive or in the sex-linked recessive form.

Autosomal recessive inheritance:
See tables 1, 2, 3, 4

Sex-linked recessive inheritance:
See tables 5, 6, 7, 8

A white face white cockatiel mutation—a rather rare mutation—and easily distinguished from a white cockatiel (see page 141).

Pied (Harlequin or Variegated)

Table 1: The pied mutation is autosomal recessive.

Parents			Young	
Male		Female	Males	Females
gray	×	pied	50% gray/pied	50% gray/pied
pied	×	gray	50% gray/pied	50% gray/pied
gray/pied	×	gray	25% gray/pied; 25% gray	25% gray/pied; 25% gray
gray	×	gray/pied	25% gray/pied; 25% gray	25% gray/pied; 25% gray
gray/pied	×	pied	25% gray/pied; 25% pied	25% gray/pied; 25% pied
pied	×	gray/pied	25% gray pied; 25% pied	25% gray/pied; 25% pied
gray/pied	×	gray/pied	25% gray/pied; 12½% gray; 12½% pied	25% gray/pied; 12½% gray; 12½% pied
pied	×	pied	50% pied	50% pied

149

Silver

Table 2: **The silver mutation is autosomal recessive.**

| Parents | | | Young | |
Male		Female	Males	Females
gray	×	silver	50% gray/silver	50% gray/silver
silver	×	gray	50% gray/silver	50% gray/silver
gray/silver	×	gray	25% gray/silver; 25% gray	25% gray/silver; 25% gray
gray	×	gray/silver	25% gray/silver; 25% gray	25% gray/silver; 25% gray
gray/silver	×	silver	25% gray/silver; 25% silver	25% gray/silver; 25% silver
gray	×	gray/silver	25% gray/silver; 12½% silver, 12½% gray	25% gray/silver; 12½% silver, 12½% gray
gray/silver	×	gray/silver	25% gray/silver; 12½% gray; 12½% silver	25% gray/silver; 12½% gray; 12½% silver
silver	×	silver	50% silver	50% silver

(left) A white face pied cockatiel.

(right) The white face cockatiel is an autosomal recessive mutation. In the U.S. this fascinating mutation was originally called "charcoal" because of the sooty appearance.

White Face (Charcoal)

Table 3: The white face mutation is autosomal recessive.

Parents			Young	
Male		Female	Males	Females
gray	×	white face	50% gray/white face	50% gray/white face
white face	×	gray	50% gray/white face	50% gray/white face
gray/white face	×	gray	25% gray/white face; 25% gray	25% gray/white face; 25% gray
gray	×	gray/white face	25% gray/white face; 25% gray	25% gray/white face; 25% gray
gray/white face	×	white face	25% gray/white face; 25% white face	25% gray/white face; 25% white face
white face	×	gray/white face	25% gray/white face; 25% white face	25% gray/white face; 25% white face
gray/white face	×	gray/white face	25% gray/white face; 12½% gray; 12½% white face	25% gray/white face; 12½% gray; 12½% white face
white face	×	white face	50% white face	50% white face

White face pearl cockatiel (front and back). Look at the even design on "both sides" of the back. No wonder this cockatiel mutation became a champion at various national and international bird shows!

Fallow

Table 4: **The fallow mutation, which is autosomal recessive, is very similar to the sex-linked cinnamon. The main difference is that adult fallows have red eyes.**

Parents			Young	
Male		Female	Males	Females
gray	×	fallow	50% gray/fallow	50% gray/fallow
fallow	×	gray	50% gray/fallow	50% gray/fallow
gray/fallow	×	gray	25% gray/fallow; 25% gray	25% gray/fallow; 25% gray
gray	×	gray/fallow	25% gray/fallow; 25% gray	25% gray/fallow; 25% gray
gray/fallow	×	fallow	25% gray/fallow; 25% fallow	25% gray/fallow; 25% fallow
fallow	×	gray/fallow	25% gray/fallow; 25% fallow	25% gray/fallow; 25% fallow
gray/fallow	×	gray/fallow	25% gray/fallow; 12½% gray; 12½% fallow	25% gray/fallow; 12½% gray; 12½% fallow
fallow	×	fallow	50% fallow	50% fallow

(left) A wonderfully colored and marked white face pearl fawn cockatiel—again, many times a top winner at bird shows!

(right) A pied white face cockatiel.

Pearl (Laced or Opaline)

Table 5: The pearl mutation is sex-linked recessive. After 6 to 12 months the males molt into normal gray adult plumage. The females retain their pearl markings.

Parents			Young	
Male		*Female*	*Males*	*Females*
gray	×	pearl	50% gray/pearl	50% gray
pearl	×	gray	50% gray/pearl	50% pearl
gray/pearl	×	gray	25% gray/pearl; 25% gray	25% gray; 25% pearl
gray/pearl	×	pearl	25% gray/pearl; 25% pearl	25% gray; 25% pearl
pearl	×	pearl	50% pearl	50% pearl

(left) One of the author's beautiful mutations: a pearl cockatiel. The pearl mutation, first bred in the 1960s in Europe, may have either relatively dark or pale yellow areas in their pearled plumage. Male birds revert to normal gray after their first molt.

(right) A yellow cheek fawn cockatiel; a very special and rather rare bird!

Cinnamon (Fawn or Isabelle)

Table 6: The cinnamon mutation is sex-linked recessive. Cinnamons, like the autosomal recessive fallows, are born with red eyes. However, the cinnamons get dark eyes within a week, whereas the fallows retain their red eyes.

Parents			Young	
Male		*Female*	*Males*	*Females*
gray	×	cinnamon	50% gray/cinnamon	50% gray
cinnamon	×	gray	50% gray/cinnamon	50% cinnamon
gray/cinnamon	×	gray	25% gray/cinnamon; 25% gray	25% gray; 25% cinnamon
gray/cinnamon	×	cinnamon	25% gray/cinnamon; 25% cinnamon	25% gray; 25% cinnamon
cinnamon	×	cinnamon	50% cinnamon	50% cinnamon

(left) A yellow cheek cockatiel, far from common.

(right) A pied female cockatiel with quite some yellow in her plumage. Nature is full of surprises!

Lutino

Table 7: **The lutino mutation is sex-linked recessive.**

Parents			Young	
Male		Female	Males	Females
gray	×	lutino	50% gray/lutino	50% gray
lutino	×	gray	50% gray/lutino	50% lutino
gray/lutino	×	gray	25% gray/lutino; 25% gray	25% gray; 25% lutino
gray/lutino	×	lutino	25% gray/lutino; 25% lutino	25% gray; 25% lutino
lutino	×	lutino	50% lutino	50% lutino

Albino

Table 8: **The albino mutation is sex-linked recessive.**

Parents			Young	
Male		Female	Males	Females
gray	×	albino	50% gray/albino	50% gray
albino	×	gray	50% gray/albino	50% albino
gray/albino	×	gray	25% gray/albino; 25% gray	25% gray; 25% albino
gray/albino	×	albino	25% gray/albino; 25% albino	25% gray; 25% albino
albino	×	albino	50% albino	50% albino

The perfect pair!

Table 9: The four possible mutation × mutation crossing combinations

Male		Female
sex-linked recessive	×	sex-linked recessive
sex-linked recessive	×	autosomal recessive
autosomal recessive	×	sex-linked recessive
autosomal recessive	×	autosomal recessive

Crossing Mutations: Some Interesting Combinations

Table 10: For crossings not shown above, simply substitute for a corresponding mutation. For example, to determine the result of cinnamon × albino, replace lutino female (in the second line of the Table) with albino. The young males will be 50% gray cinnamon/albino, the young females, 50% cinnamon.

Parents			Young	
Male		*Female*	*Males*	*Females*
sex-linked recessive	×	*sex-linked recessive*		
lutino	×	pearl	50% gray/lutino/pearl	50% lutino
cinnamon	×	lutino	50% gray/cinnamon/lutino	50% cinnamon
lutino	×	cinnamon	50% gray/lutino/cinnamon	50% lutino
cinnamon	×	pearl	50% gray/cinnamon/pearl	50% cinnamon
sex-linked recessive	×	*autosomal recessive*		
lutino	×	pied	50% gray/lutino/pied	50% lutino/pied
pearl	×	pied	50% gray/pearl/pied	50% pearl/pied
cinnamon	×	silver	50% gray/cinnamon/silver	50% cinnamon/silver
pearl	×	fallow	50% gray/pearl/fallow	50% pearl/fallow
autosomal recessive	×	*sex-linked recessive*		
pied	×	pearl	50% gray/pied/pearl	50% gray/pied
silver	×	lutino	50% gray/lutino/silver	50% gray/silver
white face	×	lutino	50% gray/lutino/white face	50% gray/white face
silver	×	pearl	50% gray/pearl/silver	50% gray/silver
autosomal recessive	×	*autosomal recessive*		
silver	×	pied	50% gray/silver/pied	50% gray/silver/pied
pied	×	silver	50% gray/silver/pied	50% gray/silver/pied
white face	×	pied	50% gray/white face/pied	50% gray/white face/pied

Crossing Mutations

The crossing of mutations is a little more complicated, but even here we have a few simple formulas. To do this, we must bring the autosomal recessive and the sex-linked recessive forms together. There are four possibilities, as shown in Table 9. Examples of each of these combinations are given on page 156. To determine what you can obtain from a certain pairing, use the formula or check Table 10.

Additional Considerations

There are two important points that apply to everything discussed in this chapter. The first is that all of the percentages given for results are *averages:* Do not expect to find the young to be 50 percent cocks and 50 percent hens in every nest. The second point is that the results of these formulas will be correct only if you know precisely the genetic makeup of the parents and how the colors are passed on. If different results should arise from those given in the formulas, then you have an unknown hidden color factor in one (or both) of the parents.

There are certain color forms that are not connected with inheritance. Frequently, this happens when birds with slight differences are bred selectively over a long period of time. Consider, for example, the red-bellied turquoisine parakeet and the

(top) A pet white face white cockatiel.

(bottom) A female yellow cheek fawn cockatiel. Once you have established a certain mutation you can start "playing" with various options as the previous pictures have shown us.

red-bellied splendid parakeet. These are produced by breeding birds that have a lot of red in their plumage.

Chapter Eight

Understanding Cockatiels

Physical Characteristics

The wild cockatiel is 11½ to 13½ inches (29–34 cm) in length, including the 6¾-inch (17-cm) tail. Both cock and hen are mainly slate gray in color, with a little shimmer of brown on the underside. Forehead, face, throat, and cheeks of the adult male are lemon yellow, running into white; the pointed crest, which is usually carried erect but can be lowered, is also lemon-yellow, turning to grayish yellow at the tip. The ear coverts are a very prominent deep orange. Also conspicuous are the bird's white shoulder patches, white greater wing coverts, and white-topped medium wing coverts. The rump, upper tail coverts, and central tail feathers are a lighter gray than the slate gray of the upper body. The underside of the tail and the lateral tail feathers are dark gray. The beak is dark gray, the feet are light gray, and the iris is dark brown.

The adult hen has gray plumage similar to that of the cock, but her yellow face is much lighter and washed with gray. The white patch of the wing coverts is smaller. The orange ear coverts are less intensively colored and somewhat smaller. The upper back, lower back, and rump are light gray with horizontal, narrow, white barring. The central tail feathers are lighter gray, with horizontal white and yellow barring; the outermost tail feathers are light yellow barred with gray; the remaining lateral feathers are light gray with conspicuous yellow-white stripes. There is a yellow-white spot on the inner webs of the flight feathers.

The gray color of the birds offers an excellent camouflage. When foraging on the ground or perched on dead trees or dead limbs, cockatiels are difficult to spot.

There are no subspecies recognized, which is to be expected in such highly nomadic birds. However, the cock birds in Queensland are substantially darker in color than those from elsewhere, a fact that at one time led ornithologists to believe they were a distinct race.

According to the well-known Australian parrot authority Joseph

Forshaw, an adult male weighs between 2¾ and 3½ ounces (80–102 g); an adult hen weighs between 3⅛ and 3¼ ounces (89–92 g). In other words, the cocks are somewhat more sturdily built than the hens.

Young cockatiels of both sexes are at first remarkably similar to the adult hen, though the young males may show some lighter yellow in the face than the young females; the orange ear coverts will also be somewhat brighter. At about six months of age, the young cocks will have their full head colors, but the barred markings of the tail, rump, and back will remain until after the first complete molt.

Feathers

In addition to giving birds the ability to fly, feathers are also necessary to help conserve the birds' relatively high body temperature, which is around 107.6°F (42°C). If we look carefully, we will observe that the soft down feathers next to the skin hold tiny pockets of air that are warmed by the body, providing excellent insulation. Exterior guard feathers are arranged over these down feathers and have the contrasting function of preventing cold air from gaining access to the skin. These outer feathers are usually covered with a thin layer of water-repellent powder. The powder layer prevents (rain)water from gaining access to the skin through the feathers, which otherwise would have a dangerous cooling effect on the insulation system.

It is a fact that young birds, whether still in the nest or after leaving it, have a lower body temperature than adult birds, so that at night or on cold days, it is necessary for them to be kept warm by the parents. Even youngsters that have left the nest are more susceptible to cold than adult birds.

Feathers are also important for other reasons, although this is not so clear in cockatiels and other parrot-like birds as it is in peafowl, duck, birds-of-paradise, weavers,

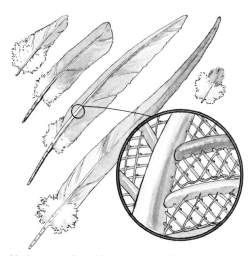

Various small and large contour feathers of the cockatiel. The tip (left) is called the inferior umbilicus, followed by the quill or calames and fluffy down. On each side of the central rachis or feather shaft is an outer and inner vane. The detailed drawing shows some parallel barbs on each side of the shaft. Each barb has small filaments equipped with tiny hooks that lock into a mesh, providing the flight surface that the cockatiel needs to push against the air.

wydahs, and so on. Feathers are used in courtship prior to the breeding season and have an important function during the brooding and rearing of young. Feathers are also used as a defense against aggression. By puffing out the feathers, a bird can make itself look much larger than it really is, and a predator will frequently have second thoughts about tackling such "large" prey. Even if a predator should attack, it will often end up with just a mouthful of feathers rather than a piece of flesh!

Feathers may be divided into three major types:

Contour feathers are arranged in regular rows covering the body and contributing to the bird's general shape. A typical contour feather consists of a central, horny shaft (rachis) bearing a pair of flattened vanes made up of rows of barbs. Each barb bears a row of barbules on either side, which interlock with the barbules of adjacent barbs by means of small hooks. The barbs are thus united, ensuring a smooth unbroken surface to the vane. By constant preening, birds are able to reinterlock barbs that have become separated.

Down feathers or plumulae have a weak shaft and a crown of free barbs. The barbules lack hooks, giving them a fluffy texture and appearance. Down feathers form the sole body coverings of nestlings, and in most adult birds they lay between or below the contour feathers.

Filoplumes are small hairline feathers lacking vanes. They consist of thin layers arranged in bundles. The filoplumes are found scattered over the body among the contour feathers.

The contour feathers are further divided into flight feathers and tail feathers.

The *flight* or *wing feathers* are arranged on the wrist and carpals as well as on the elbows and shoulder. The primary (and longest) flight feathers reach out to the ends of the wings. The secondary flight feathers are arranged behind and above the primaries on the elbows and shoulders.

Tail feathers grow out of the fleshy tail stump and are always paired (from the left and right) on the tail stump. A cockatiel has six tail feathers, but other birds have from four to ten. The vertebrae in the tail stump are highly mobile, thus allowing muscular action to move the tail feathers up and down, from side to side, or to be spread and closed.

The tail is used as a rudder during flight and as a brake for landing; it may also be used as a stabilizer in walking, hopping, or climbing. The tail also plays a part in defense (being spread to make the bird look larger) and has an important function in courtship when it is spread for display; it is used as a stabilizer during copulation. When the tail is raised and spread, it exposes the cloaca to allow defecation or copulation.

The Preen Gland

The preen gland, situated on the tail stump, consists of two reservoirs or lobes, each of which contains an oily substance that consists of fatty acids, oils, and wax. This preen fluid is secreted by the gland and reaches the surface of the skin via a uropygial papule, which has two openings. Small feathers are implanted in and around the papule. Although the function of the preen gland is not completely understood, we know that the bird takes the secretion in its beak and smears it on its feathers in order to make them waterproof. Research has shown that the preening fluid promotes the production of vitamin D3 when the sun shines on the smeared feathers. During preening, the beak comes into contact with this vitamin so that, presumably, a certain amount of it is ingested. Vitamin D is, among other things, important for strong bone formation. Thus, birds that are kept in outdoor aviaries rarely have the kind of growth problems with bones, beaks, and feet that may afflict birds kept solely indoors, without access to unfiltered sunlight.

Distribution

Cockatiels are found over the whole of Australia, especially in the interior, although in recent years they have been found more and more in coastal areas. It is suspected that the majority of those found in coastal areas are escaped cage or aviary birds and their offspring. I agree with Forshaw that the cockatiels seen in Tasmania probably are escapees. I myself saw cockatiels many times in the parks of Adelaide (South Australia) in the early 1960s. The birds were instantly recognizable by their rapid flight, narrow wings, and long tail with the extra long middle feathers. I was fascinated as the birds signaled my approach with loud calls, then flew lightning fast from the ground—where they had been seeking all kinds of seeds and berries—and perched on telegraph and electrical wires.

The species is not fully protected in Queensland, and farmers organize regular shoots to cull large numbers of the birds that may threaten their crops. In northern Victoria, I found cockatiels to be less abundant than elsewhere.

Australia: The Cockatiel's Native Land

Australia is similar in size to the United States (without Alaska) and has a long coastline that borders on three oceans and four seas.

Most of Australia has a subtropical climate, with a tropical climate in the north and a temperate climate in the south. Approximately 60 percent—especially the vast central plains—has an annual rainfall of less than 9¾ inches (250 mm). Toward the coast there is a gradual increase in rainfall. The north is influenced by seasonal monsoon rainfall and parts are covered with thick rain forest. Naturally, plant life and animal life are strongly influenced by the amount of rainfall.

Australia and the Pacific Islands form one of the most unusual

In Australia the cockatiel is very common, and when seen as dark silhouettes against the sky they look a little like Australian sparrow hawks. Their good flight capabilities are due to their narrow, slender wings and the long tail that has extremely long central feathers.

biological regions of the world. This is due to a long period of isolation from the other continents. Australia has been surrounded by oceans for at least 50 million years. During this time, many unique plant and animal species of all conceivable types have evolved, such as kangaroos, koalas, marsupial rats, marsupial wolves, lyre birds, emus, banksias, and, of course, cockatiels.

The Cockatiel in the Wild

Together with the budgerigar *(Melopsittacus undulatus)* the cockatiel is the most widely distributed hookbill on the Australian continent. The birds mainly live in open terrain marked by groups of trees and shrubs and in farmland, orchards, riverine forest, acacia shrubs, spini-

fex, plains, and roadsides. Despite the dry climate, they are generally not too far away from a water supply. Cockatiels are not bound to a particular area. Many, like budgerigars, are nomadic (especially in the north of Australia). They are constantly moving from place to place in search of food and water. In and around Darwin (especially in the winter), cockatiels tend to stay put, but in the south, they are affected by the seasonal changes, and become migratory.

Wild cockatiels usually live together in groups averaging 12 to 100 birds, but occasionally single pairs have been observed. The birds are found in various habitats, ranging from thick woodland to open savanna or semidesert grasslands. After the breeding season and when food is plentiful, the birds may gather in flocks of many hundreds, often in the company of budgerigars. When there are shortages of food, some young birds may be driven out of the home range by the older ones. In such cases, large swarms of cockatiels may appear in coastal areas where they do not normally occur. However, after a few weeks or months, they will return inland. Occasionally a few pairs will settle in the new areas and start new "colonies." In the last few decades, cockatiels have become more common in many of the coastal areas from which they

The cockatiel is the only representative belonging to the genus Nymphicus. *Because of its crest, the little cere on the bill, and the cheek markings, one could place it in the cockatoo group, while its slender shape points to a close relationship with the rosella species. In fact, the cockatiel is somewhere between these two groups, though recently the tendency has been to place this charming bird closer to the cockatoos. This picture shows the cockatiel's habitat in Queensland.*

were formerly absent. The presumably steadily increasing aridity of the inland regions and the loss of trees must be at least partly responsible for this change.

Cockatiels spend a large part of the day on the ground searching for all kinds of food. Although they are primarily dependent on the seeds of acacia and spinifex grass, they are also opportunist feeders on berries and other fruits, nectar, and even insects. I have observed cockatiels in paddocks ardently seeking grain. In this context, it must be said that cockatiels are responsible for damage to sorghum crops, though Australian farmers and ranchers do not normally regard them as serious pests.

Cockatiels like to drink in the early mornings and again in the evenings. I have seen them many times standing in shallow water at the margins of a river or creek. During the day, especially in the hot midday hours, the birds frequently rest lengthwise along dead tree branches. Their plumage colors blend with the branch and provide excellent camouflage. In captivity, cockatiels may also sit lengthwise along their perches, especially on warm days.

In this context it is worth reading what John Gould had to say about them: "During the summer of 1830 it [the cockatiel] was breeding in all of the apple-tree *(Angophora)* flats on the upper Hunter, as well as on all similar districts of the Peel, and other rivers that flow on the north-west. I have seen the ground quite covered by them while engaged in producing food, and it was no unusual circumstance to see hundreds together on the dead branches of gum trees in the neighborhood of water, a plentiful supply of which would appear to be essential to their existence."

Today, cockatiels remain somewhat tame and trusting, allowing one to approach within a few yards. They then fly swiftly, directly, and noisily to the nearest trees, where they remain for a few minutes before returning to the ground to resume their search for grass seeds, grains, berries, fruits, insects, and so on. Many times in the early mornings or late evenings, I have seen cockatiels in trees engaged in mutual preening—something one rarely sees in a large aviary.

In flight, the birds keep contact with each other through their prolonged rolling "kweel-kweel" or "kweelo-kweelo" calls. However, when foraging on the ground or sitting in a tree, they are remarkably silent. They are often in the company of red-rumped parrots *(Psephotus haematonotus)*.

Flight

Cockatiels are recognized by their graceful, straight, and swift flight. They are one of the fastest flyers among the Australian parrots. During flight, their white wing patches are remarkably conspicuous and give an indication of why cockatiels are still often referred to as cockatoo-parrots. It is thought that the white patches enable the birds to keep track of each other so that flocks can more easily stay together. When landing, a cockatiel falls to earth like a stone, checking its fall only at the last possible moment. The white shoulder patches are also plainly visible during this fall.

In spite of their rapid flight, cockatiels are still a fairly tempting target for birds of prey. No wonder these little birds approach a waterhole carefully, making many swoops to the left and to the right as they examine the area for signs of danger. If no enemies are in sight, they dive to the water surface and snap up drops of water. Although they do not appear to stand on the banks of watercourses to quench their thirst, they will land in shallow water, drink quickly, and depart rapidly, the whole process taking about seven seconds!

It is interesting to note here that cockatiels can go for a relatively long time without water. Research is beginning to indicate that cockatiels can withstand periods of drought better than any other parrot-like birds (with the sole exception, perhaps, of the budgerigar).

Breeding

In the wild, cockatiels breed mainly from August through November/December, depending on the

Quite a few aviculturists still prefer the normal gray or wild-colored bird, which, indeed, is very hard to beat!

A young white face cockatiel, asking for attention.

prevailing weather conditions. In the milder parts of New South Wales and Queensland, they may even breed from April to July or August.

Cockatiels nest in hollow limbs or in holes in the trunks of (mainly) eucalyptus trees. Many trees in the Australian bush are hollowed out by the actions of various termite species, which do not kill the tree but work on the "dead" inner wood of trunks and limbs. These insects thus play an important role in the ecology of wildlife. Cockatiels could not survive in such great numbers were it not for the quantity of nesting opportunities provided by the termites.

Usually, cockatiels nest in trees that are close to watercourses or even in the water itself (after flooding)—probably for reasons of security. The cockatiel would not win any prizes for interior decoration with regard to its nest. Generally, a little decayed wood at the base of the nest-hole is all that is required as a bed for the eggs, usually five in number but ranging from two to eight. They are white in color, with a very slight gloss, and broad elliptical in shape, measuring an average 1 by $\frac{3}{4}$ inches (24.5 × 19.0 mm). In the wild, the incubation time averages 19 days, but the time may vary depending on weather conditions. The female broods the eggs from late afternoon to early morning, when the cock takes over. Both sexes are very conscientious in their duties. This brooding by both sexes is almost unique in the world of parrots; only some cockatoos and brush-tongues (lories and lorikeets) share this habit.

I have observed several times that a wild cockatiel will take a bath before commencing its brooding shift. This has the effect of adding moisture to the nest chamber so that a certain humidity is maintained in the nest material and around the eggs. (It is for this reason that I recommend that captive-breeding birds have adequate bathing facilities.)

Wild cockatiels will accept extremely small nest cavities—sometimes not more than a fist-sized hole in a branch no thicker than one's arm. In such cases, the bird will carefully, almost elegantly, step tail-first into the nest. Such behavior may also occur in large aviaries, though this by no means indicates that the nest boxes are too small. On the other hand, I must say I have never seen wild cockatiels back tail-first into a hollow of adequate size; in other words, if they have enough room, they enter in the normal, head-first manner.

Another fascinating aspect of cockatiel behavior is the unique courtship dance of the cockbird. After he shows off his white shoulder patches, he drums his feet on the ground or on a tree branch in front of the hen. If the hen flies off, the cock will follow, stand in front of his love, and again flash his shoulder patches and drum his feet. Sadly, I have rarely seen such behavior in cage or aviary. Not all cocks in the wild have a similar degree of sex drive. Some birds will make a great show of drumming their feet on the ground or on a branch, while others leave out the fancy footwork altogether.

The Cockatiel in Scientific Literature

The cockatiel was first described by a European in 1788, when Gmelin used the scientific name *Psittacus novae-hollandiae*—an appropriate designation, since Australia at the time was known as New Holland. Eighteen years earlier, in 1770, the English explorer Captain James Cook had brought the (unfortunately damaged) specimen skin of a cockatiel to the British Museum in London. As the cockatiel was discussed in various technical publications, its scientific name was changed several times. Kerr, for example, changed it to *Psittacus hollandicus* in 1792, while Wagler renamed it *Nymphicus hollandicus* in 1832. Naturally, this caused a great deal of confusion among aviculturists.

In Volume X of the *Naturalist Library* (c. 1840), the cockatiel was described as a red-cheeked nymphicus with the scientific name of *Nymphicus novae-hollandae*. The short description of the bird was accompanied by an excellent hand-drawn illustration. The first volume of Cassell's *Book of Birds,* published toward the end of the nineteenth century, states that many hundreds

A pied white face cockatiel.

names, "Weero" and "Cockatoo-Parrot" were included.

The English name cockatiel—which is also used by American fanciers—originates from the Portuguese word *Cocatilho,* which means "small parrot." German fanciers call the bird *Nympensittich,* obviously taken from the scientific name (the word *Sittich* means "parakeet"). In Australia, there have been many different names for the cockatiel, often derived from the aboriginal native words. "Quarrion" is probably the most well known and widely used name for the bird in Australia. During my studies in Australia (1964–1967, 1981–1983, and 1994–1997), many fanciers did not know what I was talking about when I mentioned "cockatiels"!

The genus *Nymphicus* contains only one species, *Nymphicus hollandicus,* and no subspecies. Frequently, the cockatiel is regarded as a sort of link species between the cockatoos *(Cacatuidae)* and the "true parrots" *(Psittacidae).* Although most ornithologists now believe the cockatiel should be placed with the cockatoos, it is instructive to review the several characteristics shared by both cockatiels and "true parrots."

• Long, narrow tail composed of feathers arranged in "steps."

• Slender body form.

• Head scratching by placing the foot over the wing (cockatoos place the foot under the wing).

• Taking food in the beak and never holding it in the foot. (In this context,

of cockatiels had been exported to Europe. (The birds in question were, however, not cockatiels but corellas.) In the early 1920s, the British newspaper *Cage and Aviary Birds* (which is still in circulation today) published a booklet describing a "cockateel" with the scientific name *Calopsittacus novae-hollandiae.*

In the 1930s, Allen Silver's *The Parrot Book* described the cockatiel under the scientific name of *Leptolophus hollandicus.* The same English and scientific name was used in *Birds of Western Australia,* written by D. L. Serventy and H. M. Whittell and published in 1948. A fifth edition, published in 1976, still used the same names, though two further

cockatiels are similar to the large Australian group of flat-tailed parakeets *(Platycercidae),* which are always included in the *Psittacidae.*)

• Youngsters make vehement head movements as they are fed by their parents.

In contrast, there are a number of points that would appear to indicate a closer relationship with the cockatoos *(Cacatuidae):*

• The obvious, pert crest, which can be raised and lowered. (The crest is often raised and lowered when the bird sits on the cage wire and "talks" to its owner.[1])

• Cockatiel hens (and some cockatoos) have transverse stripes across the underside of the tail feathers.

• Cock and hen brood alternately.

• Cock does not feed the hen with regurgitated food; this is not necessary as both sexes feed the young.

• Gray, white, and yellow colors do not occur in adult *Psittacidae* but do occur in some cockatoos.

• The distinctive orange ear patch of the male cockatiel can be compared with that of some cockatoos; for example, the male gang-gang, red-crowned, or helmeted cockatoo *(Callocephalon fimbriatum)* has a

similar but red cheek-patch that is barely discernible in the hen. The hen cockatiel has a more somber patch than the male, but it is still conspicuous.

• When drinking, both birds make a sweeping movement with the beak, after which the head is held backward.

• When eating, both birds make similar sounds. The young make violent nodding movements when being fed. (As mentioned before, the young are fed by the adult regurgitating food from its crop with a pumping motion; this is similar behavior to that seen in pigeons and doves!)

• The first down feathers of the young are yellow and not white or gray, as is the case with most parrots. In addition, the down feathers of cockatoos and cockatiels are not shed, but develop into "powder feathers," which later produce the waterproofing talcum-like substance previously mentioned. (A similar feather development occurs in doves and pigeons, which also produce powder to protect themselves from the elements.)

• First plumage is totally changed at the first molt.

Exceptions to some of the above points have been observed. The well-known English avian veterinarian and aviculturist, Dr. G. A. Smith, kept cockatiels for some time and made notes of their behavior. He had one cock that regularly fed its mate. Another cockatiel lifted food to its mouth on its foot. Nevertheless, taking all of the above points into

---

[1]There is a small species of parrot with a crest, the horned parakeet *(Eunymphicus cornutus)* from New Caledonia and Ouvea (Loyalty Islands). However, this parrot cannot move its crest feathers, although it is similar in build to the cockatiel. This bird is protected under the Washington Convention, but may still be regularly seen in the better zoos and bird parks. See *Hand-feeding and Raising Baby Birds* (Barron's Educational Series, Inc., 1996), page 36.

The white face cockatiel has become one of the most popular mutations of this century.

consideration, it is not surprising that Joseph Forshaw regards the cockatiel to be in a subfamily *(Nyphicinae)* of the cockatoos *(Cacatuidae).*

How Cockatiels Came to Europe and the United States

It is almost certain that the first cockatiels were kept in European aviaries and cages during the late nineteenth century. Various books mentioning them were published around this time. Between 1884 and 1887, for example, the English medical doctor, W. T. Greene, published a three-volume work under the title *Parrots in Captivity.* In the first volume, the cockatiel was amply described under the scientific name *Psittacus novae-hollandiae.* Among the many interesting passages in this work was the following observation:

"Taken, when about half-fledged, from the nest, and brought up by hand, or rather by mouth, the young male Cockatiel becomes the most charming pet that can be imagined; in point of fact there is scarcely any accomplishment that he cannot be taught; he will perform all manner of little tricks, such as kissing his mistress, pretending to be dead, flying out of the window, and returning at the word of command; and he will also learn to repeat, with great distinctiveness, not only words, but short sentences, and even to imitate, in a disconnected and rambling fashion it is true, the chattering of his compatriot, the Budgerigar, or the warbling of his rival the Canary."

The Australian government instituted a strict ban on the export of native birds in 1894, so the cockatiels in Europe and the Americas are almost all derived from captive breeding. In spite of this restriction, cockatiels continued to gain popularity among aviculturists.

In the early 1920s another book about cockatiels in captivity was published in England, *Budgerigars and Cockateels,* by C. P. Arthur. This book's color descriptions of the two sexes are almost identical to those given in the work of John Gould, who conducted many remarkable ornithological studies in Australia before he returned to England in 1840. Gould called the cockatiel "Cockatoo parrot," a name that was thereafter generally used for some time. C. P. Arthur also took the natural history of the cockatiel from Gould's work, but made it obvious that he had himself kept cockatiels in his aviaries. *Foreign Birds for Beginners* by Westley T. Page, published in the early 1920s, also dealt comprehensively with the cockatiel. This reinforces the fact that the cockatiel was regarded as a popular bird that posed few difficulties in its care and management.

In 1926 the editor of *Cage and Aviary Birds,* David Seth-Smith, FZS, published his book *Parakeets, a Handbook to the Imported Species,* which soon became the standard work on the subject and was reprinted several times. According to Seth-Smith, "with the exception of the Budgerigar *(Melopsittacus undulatus),* the Cockatiel is by far the commonest Australian Parakeet with English aviarists, and scores are reared in this country annually. . . . The Cockatiel is not a specially interesting bird in captivity, being wild and noisy, and the young birds are exceedingly foolish creatures, dashing wildly about the aviary and screeching loudly on anyone's

At bird shows prizes are awarded to birds that best exemplify the standards established for the species by the various bird clubs and societies.

entrance; nevertheless, for the novice in aviculture who wishes to commence with a hardy species, there is perhaps no more suitable bird than this."

At the present time, cockatiels are extremely popular in the United States, probably owing to the many interesting color variants that are available as well as the birds' pleasant and companionable personalities. They are kept not only in aviaries but also in individual cages, as house pets. In the latter case, their ability to learn tricks and to imitate words and sounds is a strong factor. Thus, the cockatiel, with its charm and attraction to young and old, has deservedly become one of the most popular cage and aviary birds.

The American Cockatiel Society (ACS) Show Standard

General Conformation

The cockatiel is a long bird, with graceful proportions, but of good substance (full bodied). From the top of the shoulder curve to the tip of the wing, from the top of the skull to the vent, and from the vent to the tip of the tail (ideally) should measure 7 inches. The goal being a 14 inch bird with a 3 inch crest. The total bird being 17 inches.

Crest: Should be long (goal 3 inches), with good density, curving from the top of the cere fanning out to give fullness.

Head: Should be large and well rounded with no flat spot on top or back of the skull. Baldness will be faulted according to the degree of severity of each bird on the show bench. Our aim is for no bald spot even in lutinos. The eyes should be large, bright, and alert, and placed at midpoint between front and back of the skull. The brow should be well pronounced. When viewed from the front, the brow should protrude enough to indicate good breadth between the eyes. The beak should be clean, of normal length, and tucked in so the lower mandible is partially visible.

Cheek patches should be uniformly rounded, well defined (no bleeding), and brightly colored (especially on the males). Adult male cockatiels will have a bright, clear, yellow head, sharply defined where the yellow meets the border of the main body feathers. A deep bib is preferred. There should be no evidence of pin feathers.

Neck: Should be relatively long, have a very slight curvature above the shoulders and have a small nip above the chest area, giving the bird a graceful outline and eliminating the appearance of a *bull* neck or the *ramrod* posture of some psittacine species. An exaggerated *snake* neck would be reason for fault.

Body: The body of the cockatiel when viewed strictly from the side angle can be somewhat deceptive, as only a well-rounded outline of the chest will indicate whether the specimen has good substance. A frontal (or back) view shows more truly the great breadth through the chest (and shoulder) areas of an adult cockatiel (more prevalent in hens). It is the strong muscular development that enables the cockatiel to be such a strong flier. A cockatiel should have a high, broad, full chest (more prevalent in hens); a slender, tapering abdomen; a wide, straight back (no hump or sway); and be a large, sleek bird.

Wings: Should be large, wide, and long, enveloping most of the body from a side view. Should be held tightly to the body, close to the tail with no drooping of the shoulders or crossing of the wings. The wing patch should be wide (goal of ¾ inches at the widest point), well

Three champion birds bred by the author. By now we are sure that you are able to identify these mutations?!

defined, and clear of darker feathers. All flight feathers should be in evidence. Covert feathers should illustrate their growth pattern clearly.

Legs and Feet: Should hold the bird erect at approximately 70 degrees off the horizontal. Must grasp the perch firmly (two toes forward and two back), be clean, and claws not overgrown or missing.

Tail: The longest flights should be the extension of an imaginary line straight through the center of the bird's body. A humped back will cause the tail to sag too low, and a *swayed* back might elevate the tail higher than desired. The feathers themselves should be straight, clean, and neither frayed, split, nor otherwise out of line. All flights should be in evidence.

Condition

A bird in top condition has clean, tight feathers: no frayed or missing feathers, no half grown or pin feathers. The beak and claws must be of suitable length. There should be no unnatural roughness or scaling on the cere, beak, legs, or feet. If a bird is in good condition, it will be almost impossible to get it wet. Water will roll off like it does off a duck.

Deportment

In a good show stance, a cockatiel should indicate a central line approximately 70 degrees off the horizontal. It will present and display well on the perch.

Classifications on Types

The following categories concern specific coloration aspects of the normal and mutant cockatiels. While definition is necessary for each type, it is to be remembered that coloration is not as emphasized on the show bench as it may appear to be in the written standard. (See point standard.)

Normals: The color should be dark gray, ideally uniform in color throughout.

Pieds: The ideal pied will be 75% yellow and 25% dark gray. The goal being yellow pied markings over white pied markings. The aim being for tail and wing flights to be totally clear. The mask area should be clear, with no gray to create a *dirty* effect. Symmetry of pied markings is ideal.

Lutinos: Ideally a rich, deep buttercup yellow throughout. Long tail feathers and primary flights will not be severely faulted for being a lighter shade of yellow than the body.

Pearl Hens: Extensive *heavy* pearl markings that are well defined, uniform, and without splotching. Ideally the pearl markings will be a deep buttercup yellow.

Pearl Males: The same as for hens with less influence placed on the pearl markings. (However, Pearl males tend to lose their pearling when they become sexually mature. Cinnamon Pearl males revert to a pretty light gray; Pearl cocks to a very nice charcoal gray.)

Cinnamons: The color should be cinnamon, uniform in color throughout.

Fallows: The color should be light cinnamon with a yellow suffusion, uniform in color throughout. The eyes should be ruby or red.

Silvers: The color should be a dull metallic silver, uniform in color throughout. The eyes should be ruby or red.

White Face: Same as the normal void of all lipochrome. The mask area of the cock will be pure white.

Albinos: Will be void of all lipochrome, a pure white bird with ruby or red eyes. Primaries and flight feathers will not be severely faulted for being an off shade of white.

Cross-mutations: Will be judged by combining the color standards for all mutations involved.

Splits: Markings on split birds will not be penalized, as these represent a genetic factor of birds split to pied and are not a matter of faulty breeding. A bird showing the split mark is split to pied. It can be split to other mutations but will not show the split markings.

Bands

Double banded cockatiels will not be permissible at ACS regional or specialty shows. All other shows are governed by the club having the show. Double banded birds will be considered as untraceable with no band number recorded on the ACS show report; consequently no champion points will be awarded. Exceptions to double banding are:

(1) States that require a cockatiel to be banded with a state band will not be considered double banded providing they are banded with a traceable band.

(2) The show secretary shall verify the state-required band and mark the show report as such. The cage tag will be marked on the front upper left corner *D.B.* to designate the cockatiel is also banded with a state band.

ACS Point Standard

The ACS Point Standard has been formulated strictly as an aid for reference to both the judge and exhibitor in choosing the best birds. At show time, all birds will be judged by the comparison method, using the point standard as a guide.

Conformation: *60 points*
(1) *Size: 20 points*
Overall length of bird (ideally 14 inches) not including the crest.
(2) *Crest: 10 points*
Length and density of equal importance (ideally 3 inches).
(3) *Body Substance: 10 points*
Depth and breadth.
(4) *Proportions: 5 points*
Relationship of head size to body, to tail, to wings (ideally 7, 7, 7).
(5) *Wing Carriage: 5 points*
No drooping shoulders or crossed tips.
(6) *Tail: 5 points*
All feathers grown and in place, clean and unfrayed.
(7) *Head: 5 points*
Large and well rounded. Eyes large, bright, and alert. Brow well pronounced. Beak clean, normal length, tucked in. Cheek patches uniformly rounded, brightly colored. Bib deep.

Condition: *15 points*
Bird in obvious good health, tight feathered, and immaculate.

Deportment: *10 points*

Steadiness and posture, basically the result of thorough show training.

Color and Markings: *10 points*
(See the ACS show standard for details under each type's classification.)
(1) *Uniformity of Color: 5 points*
Uniformity in normals, lutinos, cinnamons, fallows, silvers, white face and albinos. Markings on pieds, pearls and cross mutations.
(2) *Depth of Color: 5 points*

Depth of color or degree of markings.

Caging: *5 points*
All cockatiels must be shown in ACS standard-type show cages when judged by ACS panel judges. The cleanliness of these cages and general condition in reference to upkeep will be weighed by the judge.

ACS Show Standard, courtesy of American Cockatiel Society. Reprinted with permission.

Useful Addresses and Literature

Organizations

United States
American Cockatiel Society, Inc.
9527 60th Lane North
Pinellas Park, FL 33782
http://www.acstiels.com

Association of Avian Veterinarians
P. O. Box 811720
Boca Raton, FL 33481-1720
(560) 393-8901
http://www.aav.org/aav.

National Cockatiel Society
Membership Secretary
P.O. Box 1363
Avon, CT 06001-1363
e-mail: tiels@sisna.com

American Federation of Aviculture
P.O. Box 56218
Phoenix, AZ 85079-6218
(602) 484-0931

International Aviculturists Society
P.O. Box 280383
Memphis, TN 38168
(901) 872-7612

Great Britain
The Avicultural Society
The Secretary
Warren Hill, Halford's Lane
Hartley Wintney, Hampshire RG27 8AG

The European Aviculture Council
c/o Mr. Dave Axtell
P. O. Box 74
Bury St. Edmunds, Suffolk IP30 OHS
(This organization has been formed to
protect the rights of bird fanciers in
Great Britain and Europe.)

Canada
British Columbia Avicultural Society
11784-90th Ave.
North Delta, British Columbia V4C 3H6

The Canadian Avicultural Society
32 Dronmore Ct.
Willowdale, Ontario M2R 2H5

Canadian Parrot Association
Pine Oaks R. R. #3
St. Catharines, Ontario L2R 6P9

Books

Cooke, Dulcie and Freddy Cooke: *Keeping and Breeding Cockatiels,* Blandford Press, London, New York, Sydney, 1987.

Doane, Bonnie Munro: *The Parrot in Health and Illness,* Howell Book House, New York, New York, 1991.

Forshaw, Joseph M.: *Australian Parrots,* 2nd ed., Lansdowne, Melbourne, Australia, 1988.

———: *Parrots of the World,* 3rd ed., Lansdowne, Melbourne, Australia, 1987.

Lantermann, Werner: *The New Parrot Handbook,* Barron's Educational Series, Inc., Hauppauge, New York, 1987.

Low, Rosemary: *The Complete Book of Parrots,* Barron's Educational Series, Inc., Hauppauge, New York, 1989.

Vriends, Matthew M.: *The New Bird Handbook,* Barron's Educational Series, Inc., Hauppauge, New York, 1989.

———: *The New Australian Parakeet Handbook,* Barron's Educational Series, Inc., Hauppauge, New York, 1992.

———: *Hand-Feeding and Raising Baby Birds,* Barron's Educational Series, Inc., Hauppauge, New York, 1996.

Magazines

The AFA Watchbird
P.O. Box 56218
Phoenix, AZ 85079-6218

Bird Breeder
An on-line magazine that can be accessed at
http://www.birdbreeder.com

Bird Talk
P. O. Box 57347
Boulder, CO 80322-7347

Cage and Aviary Birds
Prospect House
9-13 Ewell Road
Cheam, Surrey SM1 499
England

Index

Accessories, 21–24
Age:
　for breeding, 130
　life expectancy, 130
　at purchase, 12
Albino (mutation), 155
American arborvitae, 41
Anemia, 61
Anorexia, 100
Apple twigs, 138
Aspergillosis, 99–100
Australia, 161–162
Austrian pine, 41
Autopsy, 95
Autosomal, 148–149
Avian veterinarian, 17
Aviary, 5, 26–37
　indoor, 37
　location, 38–40
　outdoor, 26–37

Banding, 128–129
Bathing, 46–47, 130
　of chicks, 132
　water for, 77
Beak, 11, 61
　trimming of, 48
Biotin, 58
Bird clubs, 4, 177–178
Bird room, 37–38
Birds of prey, 36, 37
Blepharitis, 104
Blindness, 104
Blood loss, 106
Blue, 147–148
Boredom, 105
Box cages, 25
Bread, 52, 61, 101
Breastbone, 12
Breathing, 12
Breeding, 1, 4, 7–8, 119–131
　and egg laying, 124–127
　nest box for, 120–124. *See also* Nest box
　in the wild, 165–167

Brooder, 136
Brushlike feathers, 96
Buying, 1–18, 9–10, 12–13

Cages:
　accessories, 21–24
　box, 25
　breeding, 24–25, 120–124
　cleaning, 4, 45
　colony, 130
　description of, 17–18
　design of, 20
　"French," 21
　hospital, 95–96
　location, 38–40
　overview of, 19–20
　sand tray, 45–46
Calcium, 59–60, 63
　deposits, 12
Canary grass seed, 72, 138
Candling (eggs), 134
Cannibalism, 54, 106
Carbohydrates, 54
Carotenoid, 141
Carrots, 63
Catching, 16
Cats, 5, 36, 49, 112, 128
Cerebral infection, 109
Charcoal, 77, 151
Chickweed, 63
Children, 5–7
Cinnamon (mutation), 145–146, 154
Cleanliness, 77
Climbing rose, 41
Cloaca, 97
Clothespins, 24
Coccidia, 100
Cod-liver oil, 55, 61
Colds, 13, 100
Colon, 147–148
Common boxwood, 41
Common juniper, 41
Common privet, 42
Concentrated food, 73–74, 77
Copper, 61

Coprophagy, 60
Cuttlebone, 60, 61, 103, 130, 137

Dandelion, 63
Dangers, 50–51
Deformed feathers, 102
Diarrhea, 100–102
Diet, 18, 75, 130. *See also* Food; Nutrition
Discolored feathers, 102
Diseases, 99–116. *See also specific
     diseases*
  signs of, 94, 96–99
Distractions, 89
Distribution, 161
Dogs, 5, 49
Dominant (gene), 148
Douglas fir, 42
Droppings, 130
Drying, 47

Egg binding, 98, 102–103
Egg candler, 134
Egg food, 138
Egg pecking, 103
Eggs, 124–127, 166
  abandoned, 134
  candling, 134
  incubating, 125–127, 134–136
  shell-less (thin-shelled, "wind"), 103
Elizabethan collar, 106, 108
English hawthorn, 42
English holly, 42
Escherichia coli, 102
European elder, 42
European hornbeam, 43
European larch, 43
Evergreens, 40
Extruded diet, 75
Eyes, 97
  diseases of, 103–104

Fallow (mutation), 145–146, 152
Fats and oils, 54–55
Fat-soluble vitamins, 55–57
Fawn (mutation), 154
Feathers:
  brushlike, 96

contour, 160
cysts, 104–105
deformed, 102
discolored, 102
down, 160
filoplumes, 160
flight, 165
French molt, 108
missing, 11
molt, 111–113, 130
plucking or picking, 5, 54, 105–107
structure of, 159–161
tail, 160
Feet, 12, 35
Fenbendazole, 131
First weeks, 17–18
Fish-liver oil, 54
Fishmeal, 61
Flax seed, 69–70
Fledglings, 127, 131
Flight, 165
  feathers, 11
Food, 52–76. *See also* Diet; Nutrition
  bread, 52, 61, 103
  carrots, 63
  concentrated, 73–74, 77
  egg, 138
  fishmeal, 61
  fruit, 74
  green, 53, 62–64, 130
  milk, 52, 61, 103
  pellets, 75–76
  rearing, 73
  universal, 52, 73–74
Foster parents, 126
Fractures, 107–108
Free flight, 48
French molt, 108
Frostbite, 109
Frozen toes, 109
Fruit, 63, 74, 77

Gallbladder infection, 115
Genes, 148
Germinated seeds, 62, 65, 67–68
Giardiasis, 106
Glucose, 77

Goiter, 61, 109
Grass, 45, 49
Green food, 53, 62–64, 130
Grit, 18, 45, 60, 61, 77, 103, 130

Handling, 16
Hand-rearing, 136–140
Hatching, 127, 135
Hazel, 63, 138
Health necessities, 117–118
Healthy bird, signs of, 9–11
Heating, 31–32
Hemp seed, 69
Heredity, 141, 148–149
Heterozygous, 148
Hissing, 131
Homozygous, 148
Hospital cage, 95–96
Housing, 19–46
Hygiene, 46–48, 76

Identification, 10
Incubation:
  artificial, 134–136
  natural, 125–127
  time, 131–136
Incubator, 134
Indigestion, 101
Infertility, 125
Injuries, 99–116
Insecticides, 101
Insects, 52, 54, 74
Intestinal disorders, 12, 18
  diarrhea, 101–102
  E. coli infections, 102
Iodine, 61
Iron, 61
Isabelle (mutation), 154

Juvenile plumage, 129

Laced (mutation), 154
Lactobacillus, 18
Language, 89
Lighting:
  dimmer, 127–128
  supplemental, 31–32

Limestone, 60, 61
Linseed, 69–70
Location:
  aviary, 38–40
  cage, 38–40
Lutino (mutation), 142–144, 155
Lysine, 155

Management, 19
Medications:
  basic, 116–117
  Fenbendazole, 131
  Panacur, 131
Mice, 30, 36, 112, 114
Milk, 52, 61, 103
Millet, 72, 138
Minerals, 59–61
Missing feathers, 11
Mites, 104, 109–111
Moles, 36
Molt, 111–113, 130
  French, 108
  permanent, 112
  shock, 112
Mutations, 143–147. *See also specific
  mutation*

Nail trimming, 47
Natural selection, 133
Neglected young, 133
Nest boxes, 27, 29, 33, 35, 39, 120–124
Nesting material, 124, 130
Nestlings, 127–128
Net, 16
Niger seed, 70–71
Nordmann's fir, 43
Normal gray, 8
Nutrition. *See also* Diet; Food
  carbohydrates, 54
  fats and oils, 54–55
  protein, 52–54
  vitamins, 55–59, 133
  water, 61–62

Oats, 72–73
Obesity, 113
Obtaining cockatiels, 7–10

Oils, 54–55
Opaline (mutation), 144–145, 153
Oregon Holly-Grape, 43
Oriental arborvitae, 43
Overweight, 96–97
Owls, 36, 37, 112, 128

Pair (of cockatiels), 5
Panacur, 131
Parakeets, 26, 33
Parasites:
    external, 36, 104, 109–111, 114
    internal, 100, 116, 131
Pastel (mutation), 143
Pearl (mutation), 7, 10, 144–145, 153
Pellets, 75–76
Perches, 5, 16, 21–22, 26–27, 33, 132
Permanent molt, 112
Pests, 28
Phosphorous, 59–60
Picking feathers, 105–107
Pied (mutation), 7, 10, 144–145, 149
Pipping, 135–136
Plantings, 40–45. See also specific
    plant or tree
    poisonous, 44
Playpen, 31
Plucking:
    of feathers, 5, 54, 105–107
    of young, 107
Plumage, 157
    juvenile, 129
Poisoning, 101, 113
Polyoma virus, 102
Polyuria, 99
Preen glands, 113–114, 160–161
Preventive care, 99
Privet, 34, 42, 77
Profitability, 2–3
Protein, 52–54
Pruritis, 106
Psittacine beak and feather disease, 102
Psittacosis, 102, 114
Purchasing, 1–18, 9–10
Pure-bred, 148

Quarantine, 17

Radio, 93
Rape seed, 71
Rasping noises, 12
Rats, 30, 36, 112
Rearing, 127–128
    food, 73
    hand, 136–140
Recessive (gene), 148
Respiration, 97
Respiratory infection, 12, 130
Rest time, 49
Roundworms, 116

Safety porch, 30
Safflower seed, 71
Salmonella, 114–115
Sand, 18, 34
Sand tray, 45–46
Scaly face, 115–116
Scientific literature, 167–170
Scotch pine, 43
Screeching, 5
Seagreen (mutation), 147
Seeds:
    canary grass, 72
    description of, 53, 64–68
    flax, 69–70
    germinated, 62, 65, 67–68
    hemp, 69
    linseed, 69–70
    millet, 72
    niger, 70–71
    oats, 72–73
    rape, 71
    safflower, 71
    storing, 65
    sunflower, 71–72
    testing, 66–67
    white, 72
Sex-linked, 148
Shell-less eggs, 103
Shipping containers, 12
Shock, 99
Shock molt, 112
Shock standard, 172–176
Shrubbery, 40
Silver (mutation), 150

dilute, 147
dominant, 147
recessive, 146–147
Single cockatiel, 5, 6
Single parent, 133
Skin, 12
Sounds:
  hissing, 131
  rasping, 12
  screeching, 5
  squawking, 12
Sour crop, 116
Spinach, 63
Split (mutation), 148
Spruce, 43–44
Squawking noises, 12
Starvation, 99
Stoat, 37
Storing seeds, 65
Stress, 5
Structure color, 141
Stud book, 10
Sunflower seed, 71–72

Table scraps, 74–75
Tail, 12
Talking, 87–93
Taming, 78–87
Tape recorder, 91–93
T-bar stand, 81–82
Television, 49, 93
Temperature, 17–18, 31–32, 46, 130
Testing seeds, 66–67
Thiamine, 58
Thin-shelled eggs, 103
Threadworms, 116
Toes, 12, 35, 130
Torn muscles, 107
Toys, 20, 22–24
Training:
  bird psychology, 90–91
  first steps, 78–79
  ladder, 82–85
  outside cage, 79–81
  removing food, 86
  speech training, 87–93
  T perch, 81–82

tricks, 85–86
wing clipping, 86–87
Transportation, 13–14
Trimming:
  beak, 48
  nails, 47
  wing, 86–87
Tumors, 97
Twigs, 4, 77, 128, 133, 138

Understanding cockatiels, 158–176
Universal food, 52, 73–74

Vent, 12, 97
Ventilation, 39
Veterinarian, 17
Videotapes, 91–93
Vita-Lite, 112
Vitamin A, 55–56
Vitamin B12, 59
Vitamin C, 59
Vitamin D, 56–57
Vitamin E, 57
Vitamin K, 57
Vitamins, 55–59
  for fledglings, 133

Water, 61–62, 77
  bath, 46–47
Watercress, 63
Water-soluble vitamins, 57–59
Weasels, 36, 37, 112
Weight loss, 96–97
Wet nostrils, 97
White face (mutation), 151
  pearl, 7
White seed, 72
Whitewahsing, 35
Wild cockatiel, 162–165
Willow, 4, 34, 63, 77, 106, 138
"Wind" eggs, 103
Wire mesh, 28
Worms, 97, 116, 131
Wounds, 97

Yellow (mutation), 143–144
Young (cockatiels), 132–134